THE
GOLD BOOK
OF PRAYERS
REVISED EDITION

Published By
THE RIEHLE FOUNDATION
P.O. Box 7
Milford, Ohio 45150

Any reference herein to the apparitions at Medjugorje, is not an endorsement of the publisher who recognizes and accepts the judgment of the Holy See of Rome, in this matter.

Nihil Obstat: Rev. Edward Gratsch
                  February 21, 1989

Imprimatur: ✠ Most Rev. James H. Garland
                  Auxiliary Bishop of the Archdiocese of Cincinnati
                  February 24, 1989

Published by The Riehle Foundation
For additional copies, write:
The Riehle Foundation
P.O. Box 7
Milford, Ohio 45150

Copyright © 1989 The Riehle Foundation

Library of Congress Catalog Card No.: 88-061907

ISBN: 0-9618840-4-5

Scriptural excerpts from The New American Bible, and The Jerusalem Bible.

THE RIEHLE FOUNDATION
P.O. Box 7
Milford, Ohio 45150

1989

TABLE OF CONTENTS

I hope you enjoy this prayer book. Pat + I use it daily — the prayers are so beautiful. I feel so blessed I got to know you.

God Bless You!

Peace + Love in Christ,
Val Kelly

INTRODUCTION
by Kenneth Sommer
Society of Mary

More and more Christian people today are searching for new forms of prayer experiences. In our Catholic Church, we have a rich tradition of prayers and prayer guidelines that have come down to us through the years. Here is a rich little prayer book that opens our minds to that same rich tradition.

In it, is the hope that we can satisfy the hearts of the many faithful people reaching out to God, in a real and meaningful way; integrating that which has been valuable in the past, and still, open to a new and more total prayer experience of today.

In this year, dedicated to Mary, may all Her children join in prayer to give greater honor and glory to Her Son. To Her, this book is dedicated.

DEDICATION PRAYER

God, We adore and praise you.

Jesus, Pour out your Holy Spirit on all who use this booklet of prayers, that they may unite with you in giving praise and worship to the Father.

Holy Spirit, Fill our minds with your wisdom and our hearts with your love, so that we may reach out to the poor and the unloved, and proclaim that love of God to all those who do not know God's love and presence.

Amen.

Fr. Ken Sommer S.M.
Spiritual Advisor
The Riehle Foundation

PREFACE

This is a book about prayer. It is a book of prayer. Specifically, it details the praying of the Rosary. The rosaries detailed here are far more than the recitation of a series of prayers. It contains the Marian Rosary, in scriptural format, with meditations and hymns. It also contains the Jesus Rosary, composed of reflection, meditation, scripture, spontaneous prayer, and hymns.

Prayer groups will especially benefit from the use of these long standing forms of praying the Rosary. Though suitable for individual use, they are best adapted to group participation.

The Rosary of Jesus was introduced in the 1500's by Blessed Michael Pini, a hermit of the Sacred Hermitage of Camaldoli, Italy. It was given various indulgences by Pope Leo X, in his decree of February 18, 1516. Like many other forms of the Rosary, the Scriptural Rosary and Jesus Rosary have been more commonly used by religious orders in monasteries and convents. They are also more common in European countries.

The use of the Rosary is being renewed today, as more and more people are finding the graces and the blessings it promotes. The same is true of prayer in general. Two reasons seem obvious. First, the deplorable condition of the world today, an absolute necessity for prayer. Second, the events of Medjugorje, Yugoslavia.

Though the apparitions of Our Lady there, have not yet been officially recognized by the Catholic Church, it is recognized that Medjugorje is creating a world wide resurgence to conversion, reconcilliation, and prayer, all in an atmosphere of total inner peace. The Fatima messages, including the need for prayer and conversion, are being continued. The Rosary formats and prayers included here, are not an endorsement of the claimed apparitions, but simply a continuation of the current of prayer, sparked by the events there. It is toward this end, as a part of this resurgence, this great need for prayer, that this book is dedicated, and offered.

Fr. Gerard McGinnity, of Ireland, is the Senior Dean at the Irish National Seminary there. Fr. McGinnity recently authored a book on prayer, specifically, the prayer of the Rosary. He began with a profound meditation on both, and we quote from it here, in part. Fr. Gerard states:

"Since Our Blessed Lady, through the claimed apparitions at Medjugorje, has not only begun to personally direct prayer-groups in the parish there, but has also called for the establishment of such groups in every parish; many people who have visited Medjugorje, have come home and tried to respond by organizing themselves into praying groups.

"On my first visit to Medjugorje I met a woman leading an old cow along the road at the foot of the hill of apparitions, and in one hand she carried her beads—she was reciting the Rosary as she did her farmwork. I remember thinking as I approached her that she'd surely be embarrassed at my seeing her pray so publicly but she didn't hide the beads. She just looked at me and continued her meditation as if it were the most natural thing in the world to talk to God as she worked.

"I had just passed her by when I met another local woman driving six or seven lean sheep along the pathway and was amazed to notice that she, too, was reciting the Rosary as she walked along. She didn't rush to hide her beads. She greeted me and resumed her prayers, just like the others who often sit, beads in hand, at the doors of their little houses for a pause in the work of sewing tobacco leaves, their faces bronzed from the incessant sun beating down on their country and their toilworn hands.

"That is the power of the Rosary. No wonder Satan

has worked so hard and deviously to snatch it from the hands of Mary's children. Over the past twenty or more years we have uncritically accepted the deceitful suggestion that it is a 'boring prayer' because it is repetitive. Yet practice is proving us wrong. The fascinating development noticeable in modern prayer-trends is a widespread search for ways of meditating. In the enormous and unremitting stresses surrounding them as never before, many people, especially teenagers, are today trying to achieve physical relaxation, renew inner strength, recover a sense of direction in life, and even overcome dependencies such as drug addiction by taking up the practice of meditation.

"The Rosary, we now appreciate, is a superb prayer of the heart. It doesn't make sense to describe it as 'boring' because it is a prayer at a higher level than intelligence, the level of love. That is why someone who says 'I love the Rosary' without knowing why, has the Holy Spirit praying in his heart. The kind, old woman you see in Medjugorje praying the Rosary,—she's lost. Lost in God. Entirely absorbed in the prayer of the beads. Everything about her merges with the meditation. She has surrendered to something supremely greater. Her own identity doesn't seem to matter. . . .

"Mary's company does not disturb but rather distills our union with Jesus. Her mother's heart facilitates and fosters the saving work of her Son, never obscures it. Merged with Her motherhood, the mystery of Christ's redemption takes on its full meaning because as she stood sharing the intense pain of His sacrifice on Calvary, the vocation of the little Nazareth mother was extended to include all the scattered children of God; Mary was given to us as our Mother in the dying breath of Jesus."

May The Holy Spirit, through the intercession of His Spouse, The Blessed Virgin Mary, give to each of us, the gift of an unquenchable thirst for prayer.

THE RIEHLE FOUNDATION

ix

THE SCRIPTURAL ROSARY

The Scriptural Rosary combines the regular recitation of the rosary, with passages from scripture, said before each **Hail Mary**. The scripture passages evolve so that the story of each mystery, or decade, unfolds on a bead by bead basis. The passages also tie into the meditation given before the decade. It is a great aid for meditating on the mysteries.

Each decade is composed of the standard: **Our Father**, ten **Hail Mary's** and the **Glory Be**. The decade finishes with the Fatima prayer, *O my Jesus, forgive us our sins, save us from the fires of hell and lead all souls to heaven, especially those in most need of your mercy.*

A meditation and a prayer intention begins each decade. A suggested chorus or refrain from a hymn concludes each decade. The format is particularly well suited to prayer groups.

Prayers of the Rosary

The Apostle's Creed

I believe in God, the Father Almighty, Creator of heaven and earth; and in Jesus Christ, His only Son, our Lord; Who was conceived by the Holy Spirit, born of the Virgin Mary, suffered under Pontius Pilate, was crucified, died and was buried. He descended to the dead, the third day He rose again. He ascended into heaven, sits at the right hand of God, the Father Almighty; from thence He shall

1

come to judge the living and the dead. I believe in the Holy Spirit, the holy Catholic Church, the communion of Saints, the forgiveness of sins, the resurrection of the body, and life everlasting. Amen.

Our Father

Our Father, Who art in heaven, hallowed be Thy name; Thy Kingdom come; Thy will be done, on earth, as it is in heaven. Give us this day our daily bread; and forgive us our trespasses, as we forgive those who trespass against us; and lead us not into temptation, but deliver us from evil. Amen.

Hail Mary

Hail Mary, full of grace; the Lord is with thee; blessed art thou among women, and blessed is the fruit of thy womb, Jesus. Holy Mary, Mother of God, pray for us sinners, now and at the hour of our death. Amen.

Glory be to the Father

Glory be to the Father, and to the Son, and to the Holy Spirit, As it was in the beginning, is now, and ever shall be, world without end. Amen.

THE JOYFUL MYSTERIES

1. THE ANNUNCIATION

The Annunciation is a symbol of humility, of submission to the will of God. As Mary must have struggled with her own puzzlement at the angel's annunciation, her response melted into total acceptance of God's will, through her prayer. Through her appearances on earth, in this century, is she proclaiming our own annunciation? She asks for our submission to God.

Prayer Intention

Our Lady has always spoken of the great sin in the world; a world composed of pride and ego, that feels it no longer has need for God. She would want us to pray for humility, for submission to God's will. Let us offer this first decade of the rosary, in reparation; in reparation for all who revolt against God's will, against the call of their own conscience. Let us pray especially for the Church, for all bishops, priests and all those in religious life, that they might serve God with humility and imitate Mary, the "Model of the Church, the Mother of the Church."

Our Father...

1. The Angel Gabriel was sent from God....to a virgin betrothed to a man, named Joseph, of the House of David. The virgin's name was Mary. (*Lk*. 1:26)— **Hail Mary**...

3

2. The angel said to her: *Rejoice O highly favoured daughter! The Lord is with you. Blessed are you among women.* (*Lk.*1:28)—**Hail Mary**...

3. She was deeply troubled by his words, and wondered what his greeting meant. (*Lk.* 1:29)—**Hail Mary**...

4. The angel said to her: *Do not fear, Mary. You have found favor with God.* (*Lk.* 1:30)—**Hail Mary**...

5. *You shall conceive and bear a Son and give Him the name of Jesus.* (*Lk.* 1:31)—**Hail Mary**...

6. *Great will be His dignity and He will be called Son of the Most High. And His reign will be without end.* (*Lk.* 1:32-33)—**Hail Mary**...

7. Mary said to the angel, *How can this be since I do not know man?* (*Lk.* 1:34)—**Hail Mary**...

8. The angel answered her: *The Holy Spirit will come upon you and the power of the Most High will overshadow you.* (*Lk.* 1:35)—**Hail Mary**...

9. *The holy offspring to be born will be called Son of God.* (*Lk.* 1:35)—**Hail Mary**...

10. Mary said: *I am the servant of the Lord. Let it be done to me as you say.* With that the angel left her. (*Lk.* 1:38)—**Hail Mary**...

Glory be to the Father...
Oh My Jesus, forgive us our sins...

Suggested Hymn: (*Immaculate Mary*)

2. THE VISITATION

Mary came to Elizabeth, to visit with her relative. She came with a stirring message concerning the nearness of Our Saviour. The Incarnation of the Word was upon us. Is she visiting with us again? Giving us the same message? She, along with her Son, and her Spouse, the Holy Spirit, visit with us everyday. Do we respond as she did, by opening our hearts, our wills, to God? Listen to Mary's prayer of praise to God, "The Magnificat."

Prayer Intention

Let us pray this decade in thanksgiving; in thanks to God for coming to us through Mary. For greater recognition of her role, her acceptance to God's will.

Our Father...

1. Mary set out, proceeding in haste into the hill country to a town of Judah, where she entered Zechariah's house and greeted Elizabeth. (*Lk.* 1:39-40)—**Hail Mary**...

2. When Elizabeth heard Mary's greeting, the baby leapt in her womb. (*Lk.* 1:41)—**Hail Mary**...

3. Elizabeth was filled with the Holy Spirit. (*Lk.* 1:41)—**Hail Mary**...

4. She cried out in a loud voice: *Blessed are you among women and blest is the fruit of your womb.* (*Lk.* 1:42)—**Hail Mary**...

5. *Blest is she who trusted that the Lord's words to her would be fulfilled."* (*Lk.* 1:45)—**Hail Mary**...

6. Then Mary said: *My being proclaims the greatness of the Lord, my spirit finds joy in God my saviour.* (*Lk.* 1:46-47)—**Hail Mary**...

7. *For He has looked upon His servant in her lowliness; all ages to come shall call me blessed."* (*Lk.* 1:48)—**Hail Mary**...

8. *God who is mighty has done great things for me, holy is His name.* (*Lk.* 1:49)—**Hail Mary**...

9. *His mercy is from age to age on those who fear Him.* (*Lk.* 1:50)—**Hail Mary**...

10. Mary remained with Elizabeth about three months and then returned home. (*Lk.* 1:56)—**Hail Mary**...

Glory be to the Father...
Oh My Jesus, forgive us our sins...

Suggested Hymn (*Sing a New Song*)

3. THE NATIVITY

He is with us. The word was made flesh and now Jesus Christ is with us. What impact does that have on us today? He came not as a King, or a ruler, but as a poor infant, born in a manger, accompanied by shepherds. And to such humble beginnings, every knee must bend. What gifts do we bring? He is still with us, in all things, in all lives, the Prince of Peace. What gifts do we give? Bring joy, bring love and praise. Give your heart. Give your trust as Joseph did.

Prayer Intention

Let us pray for families, for guidance and grace to imitate the Holy Family. Let us pray for all parents and all those who care for the young. Let us pray especially for the gift of life, and all those who cherish it; for parents that they will lead their children closer to God. Let us pray for the unborn and in reparation for those who rob the unborn of the gift of life.

Our Father...

1. Suddenly the angel of the Lord appeared in a dream, and said to him: *Joseph, son of David, have no fear....It is by the Holy Spirit that she has conceived this child. (Mt.* 1:20)—**Hail Mary**...

2. *She is to have a son and you are to name him Jesus, because He will save his people from their sins. (Mt.* 1:21)—**Hail Mary**...

3. All this happened to fulfill what the Lord has said through the prophet: *The virgin shall be with child and give birth to a son, and they shall call him*

6

Emmanuel, a name which means 'God is with us.' (*Mt.* 1:22-24)—**Hail Mary**...

4. In those days Caesar Augustus published a decree ordering a census of the whole world. And so Joseph went to Judea, to David's town of Bethlehem—because he was of the house and lineage of David—to register with Mary, his espoused wife, who was with child. (*Lk.* 2:1), (*Lk.* 2:4-5)—**Hail Mary**...

5. While they were there the days of her confinement were completed. She gave birth to her first-born son and wrapped him in swaddling clothes and laid him in a manger. (*Lk.* 2:6-7)—**Hail Mary**...

6. There were shepherds in that region, living in the fields and keeping night watch....over their flocks. (*Lk.* 2:8)—**Hail Mary**...

7. The angel of the Lord appeared to them and they were very much afraid. The angel said to them: *You have nothing to fear.* (*Lk.* 2:9-10)—**Hail Mary**...

8. *I come to proclaim good news to you—tidings of great joy. This day in David's city a saviour has been born to you, The Messiah and Lord.* (*Lk.* 2:10-11)—**Hail Mary**...

9. Suddenly there was with the angel a multitude of the heavenly host, praising God and saying: *Glory to God in high heaven, peace on earth to those on whom his favor rests.* (*Lk.* 2:13-14)—**Hail Mary**...

10. They went in haste and found Mary and Joseph, and the baby lying in the manger; once they saw, they understood what had been told them concerning this child. (*Lk.* 2:16-17)—**Hail Mary**...

Glory be to the Father...
Oh My Jesus, forgive us our sins...

Suggested Hymn: (*Oh Come All Ye Faithful*)

4. THE PRESENTATION

Mary and Joseph, in compliance with the laws of their land, brought the infant Jesus to the temple for consecration to God the Father. She is still presenting Him to us, everyday. Offering her Son everyday to us, through the Mass, through His graces, His blessings. She also attempts to present us to God everyday; to dress us in holiness, goodness, obedience and humility for presentation to her Son. All of her appearances on earth have attempted to do just that. In this decade Mary's coming sorrows are revealed; for her Son, Jesus, and now for us.

Prayer Intention

Let us pray this decade for Mary's intentions. That all of her children may accept her role as intercessor in preparing us to be worthy of presentation to her Son, Our Saviour. And let us offer here, our personal intentions asking for Mary's intercession, and our own submission to God's will.

Our Father...

1. When the day came to purify them according to the law of Moses, the couple brought Him up to Jerusalem so that He could be presented to the Lord. (*Lk.* 2:22)—**Hail Mary...**

2. There lived in Jerusalem at the time a certain man named Simeon. He was just and pious....and the Holy Spirit was upon him. (*Lk.* 2:25)—**Hail Mary...**

3. It was revealed to him by the Holy Spirit that he would not experience death until he had seen the Anointed of the Lord. (*Lk.* 2:26)—**Hail Mary...**

4. He came to the temple now, inspired by the Spirit, and when the parents brought in the Child Jesus, he took Him in his arms and blessed God. (*Lk.* 2:27-28)—**Hail Mary...**

5. *Now Master, You can dismiss Your servant in peace; You have fulfilled Your word. (Lk. 2:29)*—**Hail Mary**...

6. *For my eyes have witnessed your saving deed, displayed for all the peoples to see. (Lk. 2:30-31)*—**Hail Mary**...

7. Simeon blessed them and said to Mary His Mother; *This child is destined to be the downfall and the rise of many in Israel, a sign that will be opposed. (Lk. 2:34)*—**Hail Mary**...

8. *And you yourself shall be pierced with a sword—so that the thoughts of many hearts may be laid bare. (Lk. 2:35)*—**Hail Mary**...

9. When the pair had fulfilled all the prescriptions of the law of the Lord, they returned to Galilee and their own town of Nazareth. (*Lk.* 2:39)—**Hail Mary**...

10. The Child grew in size and strength, filled with wisdom, and the grace of God was upon Him. (*Lk.* 2:40)—**Hail Mary**...

Glory be to the Father...
O My Jesus, forgive us our sins...

Suggested Hymn: (*Go Tell It on the Mountain*)

5. THE FINDING OF JESUS IN THE TEMPLE

Mary and Joseph searched in sorrow for three days before they experienced the joy of finding Jesus. What anguish there must have been over the lost child, over what might have happened to him. She is still searching today for all of her lost children. Do we see in this event, an example of the constant need to search for the lost?

Prayer Intention

Let us offer this decade for conversion. For all those who have wandered away from God; for those who have lost their faith; for those who give their life to the false gods of the world, money, materialism, and pleasure. *I, as Mother, love you all. I love you all even when you are far away from me and my Son. I ask you not to allow my heart to weep tears of blood because of the souls who are being lost in sin. Therefore, dear children, pray, pray, pray!*

Our Father...

1. And when He was twelve they went up for the celebration as was their custom. (*Lk.* 2:42)—**Hail Mary**...

2. As they were returning at the end of the feast, the Child Jesus remained behind unknown to His parents. (*Lk.* 2:43)—**Hail Mary**...

3. Thinking He was in the party, they continued their journey for a day, looking for Him among their relatives and acquaintances. (*Lk.* 2:44)—**Hail Mary**...

4. Not finding Him, they returned to Jerusalem in search of Him. (*Lk.* 2:45)—**Hail Mary**...

5. On the third day they came upon Him in the temple sitting in the midst of the teachers....All who heard Him were amazed at his intelligence and His answers. (*Lk.* 2:46-47)—**Hail Mary**...

6. And His Mother said to Him: *Son, why have You done this to Us? You see that Your father and I have been searching for You in sorrow.* (*Lk.* 2:48)—**Hail Mary**...

7. He said to them; *"Why did you search for me? Did you not know I had to be in My Father's house?* (*Lk.* 2:49)—**Hail Mary**...

8. But they did not grasp what He said to them. (*Lk.* 2:50)—**Hail Mary**...

9. He went down with them then, and came to Nazareth, and was obedient to them. (*Lk.* 2:51)—**Hail Mary**...

10. His Mother meanwhile, kept all these things in

memory. Jesus, for His part, progressed steadily in wisdom and age and grace before God and men. (*Lk. 2:52*)—Hail Mary...

Glory be to the Father...
Oh My Jesus, forgive us our sins...

Suggested Hymn: (*Here I Am Lord*)

THE
SORROWFUL
MYSTERIES

1. THE AGONY IN THE GARDEN

Jesus prayed with great intensity and anguish over His impending death. His agony, perhaps, was an inner one; a distress and sadness that the death He was about to undergo, would be suffered in vain for many. Like Jesus, we also face crucial decisions, stress and difficulty, and pain in our daily lives. In our trials and misery, will we be loyal? If we can kneel with Jesus in His agony, He will be there in ours.

Prayer Intention

Let us pray for all those who suffer, physically, and emotionally; all those who are spiritually ill. Let us pray that their agony can be united with that of Jesus, and not lost through despair or resentment. We pray that Mary, *The Comforter of the Afflicted,* might assist in laying the needs of the suffering before her Son.

Our Father...

1. Then Jesus went with them to a place called Gethsemani; and He began to experience sorrow and distress. (*Mt.* 26:36-37)—**Hail Mary...**

2. Then He said to them, *My heart is nearly broken with sorrow. Remain here and stay awake with Me.* (Mt. 26:38)—**Hail Mary...**

3. He withdrew from them and knelt down and prayed.

12

(*Lk.* 22:41)—**Hail Mary**...

4. *Father, if it is possible, let this cup pass from me. Still, let it be as you would have it, not as I.* (*Mt.* 26:39)—**Hail Mary**...

5. When He returned to His disciples, He found them asleep. He said to Peter, *So you could not stay awake with me for even an hour? Be on guard and pray that you may not undergo the test. The spirit is willing, but nature is weak.* (*Mt.* 26:40-42)—**Hail Mary**...

6. In His anguish, He prayed more earnestly. An angel appeared to Him, coming from Heaven to give Him strength. (*Lk.* 22:44-43)—**Hail Mary**...

7. *The hour is on us when the Son of Man is to be handed over to the power of evil men.* (*Mt.* 26:45)—**Hail Mary**...

8. While He was still speaking, Judas, one of the twelve, arrived accompanied by a great crowd with swords and clubs. (*Mt.* 26, 47)—**Hail Mary**...

9. He immediately went over to Jesus, said to him, *Peace, Rabbi,* and embraced Him. (*Mt.* 26:49)—**Hail Mary**...

10. Jesus answered, *Friend, do what you are here for.* At that moment they stepped forward to lay hands on Jesus and arrested Him. (*Mt.* 26:50)—**Hail Mary**...

Glory be to the Father...
O My Jesus, forgive us our sins...

Suggested Hymn:
(*I Have Loved You With an Everlasting Love*)

2. THE SCOURGING AT THE PILLAR

Pilate, disturbed at the meek majesty of his prisoner, had him scourged at the pillar, though he could not find any fault in him. Perhaps he simply resented the fact that

Jesus had no use for this world, Pilate's world, and spoke so overwhelmingly for the next world. Which way do we view this world? Are we willing to give all, only for this life? Or can we offer and accept our suffering as a sacrifice to God, as Jesus offered His life for us?

Prayer Intention

Let us offer this decade in thanksgiving for the sacrifices made by Our Lord for the love of us. Pray also, in reparation for all the sins of the world inflicted upon the Sacred Heart of Jesus, and the indifference to His Mother.

Our Father...

1. As soon as it was daybreak, the chief priests, with the elders and scribes, reached a decision. They bound Jesus, led him away, and handed him over to Pilate. Pilate interrogated him, *Are you the King of the Jews?* (*Mk.* 15:1-2)—**Hail Mary...**

2. Jesus answered, *My Kingdom does not belong to this world.* At this pilate said to Him, *So then you are a King?* Jesus replied, *It is you who say I am a King. The reason I was born, the reason why I came into the world is to testify to the truth. Anyone committed to the truth, hears my voice.* (*John* 18:36-37)—**Hail Mary...**

3. *This much only will I say, From now on, the Son of Man will have his seat at the right hand of the Power of God.* (*Lk.* 22:69)—**Hail Mary...**

4. *So you are the Son of God?* they asked in chorus. He answered, *It is you who say that I am.* (*Lk.* 22:70)—**Hail Mary...**

5. Pilate's next move was to take Jesus and have Him scourged. (*John* 19:1)—**Hail Mary...**

6. Despised and rejected by men, a man of sorrows. (*Is.* 53:3)—**Hail Mary...**

14

7. And yet, ours were the sufferings He bore. (*Is.* 53:4)—**Hail Mary...**

8. He was pierced through for our faults, crushed for our sins. (*Is.* 53:5)—**Hail Mary...**

9. They blindfolded Him, slapped Him and then taunted Him. (*Lk.* 23:64)—**Hail Mary...**

10. And after He had Jesus scourged, Pilate handed Him over to be crucified. (*Mk.* 15:15)—**Hail Mary...**

Glory be to the Father...
O My Jesus, forgive us our sins...

Suggested Hymn: (*Sweet Sacrament We Thee Adore*)

3. THE CROWNING OF THORNS

The coronation, offered to Jesus by the world, was a crown of thorns. How do we crown Him now? Do we deny Him, or simply show indifference? Do we truly seek Him out? The mockery of this pain inflicting crowning, asks us how we crown Our Saviour.

Prayer Intention

Let us offer this decade for all people who suffer under oppression and persecution. Those who suffer humiliation and rejection. And we pray in reparation to God for the sins of the world, the thorns of the crown.

Our Father...

1. The soldiers now led Jesus away into the hall known as the Praetorium; at the time they assembled the whole cohort. (*Mk.* 15:16)—**Hail Mary...**

2. They dressed Him in royal purple, then wove a crown of thorns and put it on Him. (*Mk.* 15:17)—**Hail Mary...**

3. They began to salute Him, *All hail! King of the Jews!* (*Mk.* 15:18)—**Hail Mary...**

4. Continually striking Jesus on the head with a reed and spitting at Him, they genuflected before Him and pretended to pay Him homage. (*Mk.* 15:19)—**Hail Mary...**

5. Pilate said to the crowd: *Observe what I do. I am going to bring Him out to you to make you realize that I find no case against Him.* (*John* 19:4)—**Hail Mary...**

6. When Jesus came out wearing the crown of thorns and the purple cloak, Pilate said to them, *Look at the Man!* (*John* 19:5)—**Hail Mary...**

7. As soon as the chief priests and the temple guards saw Him they shouted, *Crucify Him! Crucify Him!* (*Jn.* 19:6)—**Hail Mary...**

8. *Why, what crime has He committed?* asked Pilate. They only shouted the louder, *Crucify Him!* (*Mk.* 15:14)—**Hail Mary...**

9. Pilate said to the Jews, *Look at your King.* (*Jn.* 19:14)—**Hail Mary...**

10. In the end, Pilate handed Jesus over to be crucified. (*Jn.* 19:16)—**Hail Mary...**

    Glory be to the Father...
    O My Jesus, forgive us our sins...

    Suggested Hymn: (*Lay Your Hands*)

4. THE CARRYING OF THE CROSS

The Son of God carries the instrument of His death to the hill of Calvary. Jesus' carrying of the cross was a fulfillment of His earlier words, *Let all who would believe in me, take up their cross and follow me.* A cross he didn't have to carry. Neither do we, unless we choose Jesus over Satan and sin. Mary, His Mother states that, *Through the cross, God is being glorified in every person.*

Do not be afraid to carry it. My Son is with you and He will help you. Let us find, through the steps to Calvary, the roadway of our own lives.

Prayer Intention

Let us pray for the suffering, the lonely, the homeless. Let us ask Jesus to give special meaning to the crosses they carry.

Our Father...

1. When they had finished making a fool of Him, they stripped Jesus of the cloak, dressed Him in His own clothes, and led Him off to crucifixion. (*Mt.* 27:31)— **Hail Mary**...

2. On their way out they met a Cyrenian named Simon. This man they pressed into service to carry the cross. (*Mt.* 27:32)—**Hail Mary**...

3. A great crowd of people followed Him, including women who beat their breasts and lamented over Him. (*Lk.* 23:27)—**Hail Mary**...

4. Jesus turned to them and said: *Daughters of Jerusalem, do not weep for me. Weep for yourselves and for your children.* (*Luke* 23:28)—**Hail Mary**...

5. Two others who were criminals were led along with Him to be crucified. (*Lk.* 23:32)—**Hail Mary**...

6. Upon arriving at a site called Golgotha, (a name which means Skull Place), they gave Him a drink of wine flavored with gall, which He tasted but refused to drink. (*Mt.* 27:33-34)—**Hail Mary**...

7. When they had crucified Him, they divided His clothes among them by casting lots; then they sat down there and kept watch over Him. (*Mt.* 27:35-36)—**Hail Mary**...

8. *Whoever wishes to be my follower must deny his very self.* (*Lk.* 9:23)—**Hail Mary**...

9. *He must take up his cross each day and follow in my steps.* *(Lk. 9:23)*—**Hail Mary**...

10. *Whoever would save his life will lose it, whoever loses his life for my sake, will save it.* *(Lk. 9:24)*—**Hail Mary**...

   Glory be to the Father...
   O My Jesus, forgive us our sins...

   Suggested Hymn: *(Oh Lord I am Not Worthy)*

5. THE CRUCIFIXION

Jesus died on the cross. With it came our redemption, our salvation. Before His final breath, He gave the world His Mother, and gave her a role in the salvation of all mankind by making us all, her children. Just as she was there, at the foot of the cross, she asks us to pay at the foot of the cross. Our forgiveness is there. Great graces are there. Love the cross. In this meditation, is our salvation.

Prayer Intention

Let us pray for forgiveness and as Jesus forgave on the cross, let us pray for the grace to forgive others. Let us give all our past pain to Jesus. It is why He is on the cross.

Our Father...

1. Jesus said, *Father, forgive them, they do not know what they are doing.* *(Lk. 23:34)*—**Hail Mary**...

2. One of the criminals said: *Jesus, remember me when You enter upon Your reign.* And Jesus replied, *I assure you; this day you will be with Me in paradise.* *(Lk. 23:42-43)*—**Hail Mary**...

3. Seeing His Mother there with the disciple whom He loved, Jesus said to His Mother, *Woman, there is your son.* *(Jn. 19:26)*—**Hail Mary**...

4. In turn He said to the disciple, *There is your Mother.* From that hour onward, the disciple took her into his care. (*Jn.* 19:27)—**Hail Mary**. . .

5. Then toward midafternoon, Jesus cried out in a loud tone, *My God, My God, why have You forsaken Me?* (*Mt.* 27:46)—**Hail Mary**. . .

6. Jesus realizing that everything was now finished, said to fulfill the Scriptures, *I am thirsty.* There was a jar there, full of common wine. They stuck a sponge soaked in this wine on a stick, and raised it to His lips. (*Jn.* 19:28)—**Hail Mary**. . .

7. When Jesus took the wine, He said, *Now it is finished.* (*Jn.* 19:30)—**Hail Mary**. . .

8. Jesus uttered a loud cry and said, *Father, into Your hands I commend My spirit.* After He said this, He expired. (*Lk.* 23:46)—**Hail Mary**. . .

9. Darkness came over the whole land until midafternoon with an eclipse of the sun. The curtain in the sanctuary was torn in two. (*Lk.* 23:44-45)—**Hail Mary**. . .

10. They took Jesus' body, and in accordance with Jewish burial custom, bound it up in wrappings of cloth with perfumed oils. (*Jn.* 19:40)—**Hail Mary**. . .

Glory be to the Father. . .
O My Jesus, forgive us our sins. . .

Suggested Hymn: (*Were You There*)

THE GLORIOUS MYSTERIES

1. THE RESURRECTION

Jesus rose from the dead. With it He conquered death, defeated Satan, sin, and the world, and gave new life to mankind. The joy of the risen Christ is greater than pain. The hope that comes from His resurrection is the victory over our own fear of dying. We follow Jesus; follow His steps through this world, and into the next.

Prayer Intention

Let us pray in thanksgiving and in praise, giving glory to the risen Lord. Let us offer to the Triumphant Prince of Peace, all those in despair, those who have lost hope, lost faith; that in the Resurrection of Jesus will be their own future. He is the way and the truth and the life.

Our Father...

1. After the sabbath, as the first day of the week was dawning, Mary Magdalene came with the other Mary to inspect the tomb. (*Mt.* 28:1)—**Hail Mary**...

2. The angel came to the stone, rolled it back and sat on it. (*Mt.* 28:2)—**Hail Mary**...

3. Then the angel spoke, addressing the women: *Do not be frightened. I know you are looking for Jesus the crucified, but He is not here. He has been raised, exactly as He promised.* (*Mt.* 28:5-6)—**Hail Mary**...

4. *He has been raised from the dead and now goes ahead*

of you to Galilee. (Mt. 28:7)—**Hail Mary**...

5. On the evening of the first day of the week, even though the disciples had locked the doors of the place where they were.... Jesus came and stood before them. *Peace be with you.* He said. *(Jn.* 20:19)—**Hail Mary**...

6. In their panic and fright they thought they were seeing a ghost. *(Lk.* 24:37)—**Hail Mary**...

7. He said to them, *Why are you disturbed? Look at My hands and My feet; it is really I. (Lk.* 24:38-39)—**Hail Mary**...

8. At the sight of the Lord, the disciples rejoiced. *(Jn.* 20:20)—**Hail Mary**...

9. *Peace be with you.* Jesus said again. *As the Father has sent Me, so I send you. (Jn.* 20:21)—**Hail Mary**...

10. *I am the resurrection and the life; whoever believes in Me, though he should die, will come to life. (Jn.* 11:25-26)—**Hail Mary**...

   Glory be to the Father...
   O My Jesus, forgive us our sins...

   Suggested Hymn: (*He Is Lord, He Is Lord*)

2. THE ASCENSION

He goes to prepare a place for us, and has returned to The Father, in heaven. And He has promised: *Where I am, you can be too.* Through His ascension, He has shown us a preview of our life hereafter. The Good Shepherd guides us through the valley of darkness. We are constantly tempted, distracted, disillusioned by here-and-now needs. It is Mary who assists, frequently trying to lift us up, trying to prepare us for her Son, asking that we make Jesus the first priority in our life. *You cannot serve two masters. You cannot serve God and the money of the world. Seek first the Kingdom of God.*

21

Prayer Intention

Let us pray for direction; direction in our lives and for all those who have lost the way; that they may turn back to God. Let us pray that we might give direction to the children in the world, in meeting Jesus. Let us pray that Jesus may become their first priority.

Our Father...

1. Jesus led His disciples out near Bethany, and with hands upraised, blessed them. (*Lk.* 24:50)—**Hail Mary...**

2. Jesus addressed them in these words: *Full authority has been given to Me both in heaven and on earth.* (*Mt.* 28:18)—**Hail Mary...**

3. *Go therefore, and make disciples of all the nations. Baptize them in the name of the Father, and of the Son, and of the Holy Spirit.* (*Mt.* 28:19)—**Hail Mary...**

4. *And know that I am with you always, until the end of the world.* (*Mt.* 28:20)—**Hail Mary...**

5. *The man who believes in the good news and accepts baptism will be saved; the man who refuses to believe in it will be condemned...* (*Mk.* 16:16)—**Hail Mary...**

6. As Jesus blessed them, He left them and was taken up to heaven. (*Lk.* 24:51)—**Hail Mary...**

7. He was lifted up before their eyes in a cloud which took Him from their sight. (*Acts.* 1:9)—**Hail Mary...**

8. This Jesus Who has been taken from you will return, just as you saw Him go up into the heavens. (*Acts.* 1:11)—**Hail Mary...**

9. They fell down to do Him reverence, then returned to Jerusalem filled with joy. (*Lk.* 24:52)—**Hail Mary...**

10. Jesus took His seat at God's right hand. (*Mk.* 16:19)—**Hail Mary...**
    Glory be to the Father...

O My Jesus, forgive us our sins...

Suggested Hymn: (*His Peace is Flowing Like a River*)

3. THE DESCENT OF THE HOLY SPIRIT

Before His Ascension, Jesus had said, *Because I go, the Paraclete will come.* The Spirit of God descended upon the apostles. They were empowered with the special gifts of God, to carry on the Lord's work of redemption. With them, was Mary, and the other women, praying with the infant Church. She has never ceased to pray for us and the Church, asking her Spouse, the Holy Spirit, to again touch hearts. She has told us to pray to the Holy Spirit; that those who have the gifts of the Holy Spirit have everything.

Prayer Intention

Let us offer these prayers for our own penticost. For an increase in the Holy Spirit's gifts to us. We pray for a deeper faith, and trust in God; for a complete submission to the will of God. Let us pray especially for gifts to the young, for strength that they may be able to stand up to the deception Satan brings to their daily activities.

Our Father...

1. Jesus said, *I will ask the Father and He will give you another Paraclete, to be with you always.* (*Jn.* 14:16)—**Hail Mary...**

2. *The Paraclete, the Holy Spirit, whom the Father will send in My name, will instruct you in everything, and remind you of all that I told you.* (*Jn.* 14:26)—**Hail Mary...**

3. *Within a few days you will be baptized with the Holy Spirit.* (*Acts.* 1:5)—**Hail Mary...**

4. *You will receive power when the Holy Spirit comes down on you; then you are to be My witnesses in Jerusalem, throughout Judea....and even to the ends of the earth.* (Acts. 1:8)—**Hail Mary**...

5. When the day of Pentecost came it found them gathered in one place. Suddenly from up in the sky there came a noise like a strong driving wind, which was heard all through the house. (*Acts.* 2:1-2)—**Hail Mary**...

6. Tongues as of fire appeared, which parted and came to rest on each of them. All were filled with the Holy Spirit. (*Acts.* 2:3)—**Hail Mary**...

7. They began to express themselves in foreign tongues and make bold proclamation as the Spirit prompted them. (*Acts.* 2:4)—**Hail Mary**...

8. Staying in Jerusalem at the time were devout men of every nation. These heard the sound, and assembled in a large crowd. They were confused because each heard the disciples speaking his own language. (*Acts.* 2:5-6)—**Hail Mary**...

9. Peter stood up with the Eleven and addressed them, *You must reform and be baptized, each one of you, in the name of Jesus Christ, that your sins may be forgiven; then you will receive the gift of the Holy Spirit.* (Acts. 2:38)—**Hail Mary**...

10. Those who accepted His message were baptized; some three thousand were added that day. (*Acts.* 2:41)—**Hail Mary**...

   Glory be to the Father...
   O My Jesus, forgive us our sins...

      Suggested Hymn: (*Come Holy Ghost*)

4. THE ASSUMPTION

Mary is assumed, body and soul into heaven. Reunited with her Son, Jesus. Through her assumption, Mary became the reflection of her risen Son. She is also the model of the perfection to which we are called. She represents total submission to the will of God. Mary, as Mother of the Church, protect the Mystical Body of your Son, and our Saviour.

Prayer Intention

Here let us ask Mary to especially pray with us for the souls in purgatory; that she might join with us in intercession for those who can no longer help themselves. Those who now entirely depend on us for their final purification. Let us pray especially for the souls forgotten, who have no one to remember them.

Our Father...

1. The Lord God said to the serpent: *I will put enmity between you and the woman and between your offspring and hers.* (*Gn.* 3:15)—**Hail Mary...**

2. *He will strike at your head, while you strike at His heel.* (*Gn.* 3:15)—**Hail Mary...**

3. A great sign appeared in the sky, a woman clothed with the sun, with the moon under her feet, and on her head a crown of twelve stars. (*Rv.* 12:1)—**Hail Mary...**

4. *Father, all those you gave me I would have in my company where I am.* (*Jn.* 17:24)—**Hail Mary...**

5. Wherefore She is our Mother in the order of grace. (*Vat. I, Constit.* on Ch. 61)—**Hail Mary...**

6. Taken up to heaven, She did not lay aside this salvific duty, but by Her intercession continues to bring us the gifts of eternal salvation. (*Vat. II, Constit.* of Ch. 62)—**Hail Mary...**

7. *For He has looked upon His servant in her lowliness.* (*Lk.* 1:48)—**Hail Mary**...

8. *All ages to come shall call me blessed.* (*Lk.* 1:48)— **Hail Mary**...

9. Those who love me I also love, and those who seek me find me...He who finds me finds life, and wins favor from the Lord. (*Prov.* 8:17-35)—**Hail Mary**...

10. Come then my love. My lovely one come. (*Song* 2:10)—**Hail Mary**...

Glory be to the Father...
O My Jesus, forgive us our sins...

Suggested Hymn: (*I lift up my Soul*)

5. THE CORONATION OF MARY

Mary is crowned Queen of the angels and saints in heaven. Queen of the Holy Rosary, Queen of Peace, Queen of Apostles, Queen of Prophets. How many titles have been given to the Mother of the Incarnation of the Word! Not only is she proclaimed as the New Eve, and Mother of the Church, she is also given a prominent position in the salvation and redemption of the world. Her soul magnifies the Lord, all nations shall call her blessed. Her glorious coronation in heaven, is our hope.

Prayer Intention

Let us offer this mystery then for Mary's intentions. Her intercession, her constant appearances, her role as Mediatrix of graces. Let us pray that her efforts in our behalf, her efforts to lead all her children back to her Son, will not be impeded. We pray also, to God, The Father, in thanksgiving for Mary's presence, for her role, for her help. We pray in thanksgiving that she is.

Our Father...

1. *God who is mighty, has done great things for me. (Lk. 1:49)*—**Hail Mary...**

2. My heart overflows with a goodly theme; as I sing my ode to the king. *(Ps. 45:2)*—**Hail Mary...**

3. Fairer in beauty are you than the sons of men; grace is poured out upon your lips; thus God has blessed you forever. *(Ps. 45:3)*—**Hail Mary...**

4. Because of this gift of sublime grace, She far surpasses all creatures, both in heaven and on earth. *(Vat. II, Constit. of Ch. 53)*—**Hail Mary...**

5. I am the rose of Sharon, I am the lily of the valleys. *(Song 2:1)*—**Hail Mary...**

6. So now, O children, listen to me; instruction and wisdom do not reject. *(Prov. 8:32-33)*—**Hail Mary...**

7. The Lord chose Her. He chose Her before She was born. *(Div. off.)*—**Hail Mary...**

8. Entirely holy, and free from all stain of sin. *(Constit. of Ch. 56)*—**Hail Mary...**

9. Freely cooperating in the work of human salvation through faith and obedience. *(Constit. of Ch. 56)*—**Hail Mary...**

10. Blessed are you, daughter, by the Most High God, above all the women on earth. *(Judith 13:18)*—**Hail Mary...**

Glory be to the Father...
O My Jesus, forgive us our sins...

Suggested Hymn: *(City of God)*

Prayer After the Rosary

O, God, whose only-begotten Son, by His life, death and resurrection, has purchased for us the rewards of eternal life; grant, we beseech Thee, that, meditating upon these mysteries of the Most Holy Rosary of the Blessed

Virgin Mary, we may imitate what they contain and obtain what they promise, through the same Christ Our Lord. Amen.

May the Divine Assistance remain always with us. And may the souls of the faithful departed, through the mercy of God, rest in peace. Amen.

THE
ROSARY
OF JESUS

This ancient chaplet renews a form of prayer from centuries ago. It is rapidly spreading around the world, particularly in prayer groups and communities.

The interest in the Jesus Rosary apparently stems from the claimed apparitions in Medjugorje, where, in 1983, the visionary Jelena, reported a request from Our Lady to have a young people's prayer group formed, and use the Jesus Rosary as part of their format. These prayer groups have multiplied in Yugoslavia, and around the world.

The Rosary is said in remembrance of the 33 years of Jesus' life on earth. It consists of **The Apostles Creed**, 33 **Our Fathers** and 7 **Glory Be's**. It is divided into 7 mysteries, each inviting the individual or group, to meditate on an aspect of Jesus' life. Each division or mystery is composed of:

- **Naming and Reflecting on the Mystery.** (Scripture passages are listed here as an aid, if desired.)

- **A Special Prayer Intention for the Mystery.**

- **Meditation and Spontaneous Prayer by the Group.** (Referencing the mystery or the prayer intention.)

- **Saying 5 Our Father's.** (3 after the 7th mystery.)

- **The Ejaculation,** *O Jesus, be our strength and protection.*

- **A Verse, or Refrain from a Hymn after each Mystery.**

Following are the suggestions for each mystery, scripture passages that apply, the prayer intention, and a suggested hymn.

After the 7 mysteries there follows a meditation on the Holy Spirit, and finally, 7 **Glory Be to The Father.**

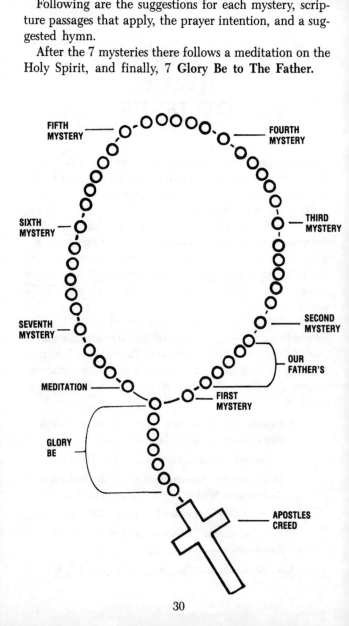

FIFTH MYSTERY

FOURTH MYSTERY

SIXTH MYSTERY

THIRD MYSTERY

SEVENTH MYSTERY

SECOND MYSTERY

OUR FATHER'S

MEDITATION

FIRST MYSTERY

GLORY BE

APOSTLES CREED

HOW TO SAY
THE
ROSARY
OF JESUS

- The Apostles Creed...

FIRST MYSTERY: *The Birth of Jesus*
(*Mt.* 1:18-25), (*Lk.* 2:16-18), (*Is.* 7:14), (*Is.* 11:1-9).

- Prayer Intention: For Peace in the World.
- Meditation and spontaneous prayer.
- **5 Our Father's...**
- *O Jesus, be our strength and protection.*

Suggested Hymn: *(His Peace is Flowing Like a River)*

SECOND MYSTERY: *Jesus' love and compassion*
for the poor and afflicted
(*Mt.* 8:14-17), (*Lk.* 7:11-15), (*Mk.* 10:46-52), (*Mk.* 1:40-45).

- Prayer Intention: For the Holy Father and the Bishops.
- Meditation and spontaneous prayer.
- **5 Our Father's...**
- *O Jesus, be our strength and protection.*

Suggested Hymn: *(City of God)*

THIRD MYSTERY: *Jesus trusted in His Father*
and carried out His will
(*Jn.* 14:1-7), (*Mt.* 26:39), (*Mk.* 14:35-36), (*Jn.* 6:32-40).

- Prayer Intention: Let us pray for priests, brothers and
  sisters and all those who serve God in a particular way.
- Meditation and spontaneous prayer.

31

- 5 Our Father's...
- *O Jesus, be our strength and protection.*
Suggested Hymn: *(All That I Am)*

FOURTH MYSTERY: *Jesus willingly came*
To earth, suffered and died,
because He loved us so much
(Rom. 15:7-13), *(Jn.* 15:9-13), *(Jn.* 10:14-18), *(Lk.* 22:39-44).

- Prayer Intention: Let us pray for families, for parents, and their children.
- Meditation and spontaneous prayer.
- 5 Our Father's...
- *O Jesus, be our strength and protection.*

Suggested Hymn: *(We Gather Together)*

FIFTH MYSTERY: *Jesus gave up His life*
as a sacrifice for us.
(Jn. 14:12-16), *(1 Tim.* 2:5-6), *(Heb.* 2:9-11), *(Rm.* 4:24-25).

- Prayer Intention: Let us pray that we too may be capable of offering our life for our neighbor.
- Meditation and spontaneous prayer.
- 5 Our Father's...
- *O Jesus be our strength and protection.*

Suggested Hymn: *(Spirit of The Living God)*

SIXTH MYSTERY: *The Resurrection of Jesus,*
His victory over Satan and death
(Mt. 4:8-11), *(1 Cor.* 15:12-19), *(Acts* 2:23-24), *(2 Cor.* 4:11-14).

- Prayer Intention: Let us pray that we may eliminate all sin from our lives so that Jesus may re-live in our hearts.
- Meditation and spontaneous prayer.
- 5 Our Father's...
- *O Jesus, be our strength and protection.*

Suggested Hymn: *(He is Lord)*

SEVENTH MYSTERY: *The Ascension of Jesus into Heaven*
(*Acts* 1:8-11), (*Heb.* 1:1-4), (*Lk.* 24:46-53), (*Jn.* 16:25-28).

- Prayer Intention: Let us pray that the Will of God may triumph, so that we may be open to the Will of God in our own lives.
- Meditation and spontaneous prayer.
- **3 Our Father's**...
- *O Jesus, be our strength and protection.*

Suggested Hymn: (*Look Beyond*)

MEDITATION

- Let us contemplate how *Jesus sent the Holy Spirit.* Let us pray that the Holy Spirit may descend upon us.

Suggested Hymn: (*Lord Send Out Your Spirit*)

- **7 Glory Be to the Father**...

Suggested Hymn: (*All People That on Earth do Dwell*)

(The Servite Rosary Of)

THE SEVEN
SORROWS
OF MARY

Meditation on the Seven Sorrows of Our Lady is a way of sharing in the major sorrows of Mary's life. As we pray one **Our Father,** seven (or one) **Hail Mary,** and one **Glory Be** for each sorrow, we ponder the pain she endured along with her Son. We ask her to help us understand the evil we have done and to lead us to repentance. By joining our sorrows with Mary's, as she joined her sacrifices with her Son's, we participate in the work of our Redemption.

An Act of Contrition

O Lord, Jesus Christ, I am truly sorry for my sins. I humbly ask Your forgiveness, and I promise with Your help to prove worthy of Your love by sharing in Your Passion and death through Our Blessed Mother's sorrows. Amen.

FIRST SORROW: *The Prophecy of Simeon*

How great was the shock to Mary's heart at hearing the sorrowful words in which Simeon foretold the bitter passion and death of her sweet Jesus. Dear Mary, obtain for me a true sorrow for my sins. . .

SECOND SORROW: *The Flight into Egypt*

Consider the sharp sorrow which Mary felt when she and Joseph had to suddenly flee by night in order to preserve her beloved Child from the slaughter decreed by Herod. What anguish was hers; how great her privations in that long journey. What sufferings she bore in that land of exile.

THIRD SORROW: *The Loss of Jesus in the Temple*

How dread was the grief of Mary when she realized that she had lost her beloved Son. Filled with worry and weariness, she and Joseph returned to Jerusalem, and for three long days sought Jesus, until finding Him in the temple.

FOURTH SORROW: *Mary Meets Jesus on the way to Calvary*

Come, O sinners, come and see if you can endure so sad a sight. This Mother, so tender and loving, meets her beloved Son amid those who drag Him to a cruel death. Consider, O dear people, the tremendous grief as their eyes met—the sorrow of the blessed mother thus beholding her Son.

FIFTH SORROW: *Jesus Dies on the Cross*

Look upon the two sacrifices on Calvary—one, the body of Jesus; the other, the heart of Mary. Sad is the sight of that dear Mother seeing her beloved Son cruelly nailed to the tree of the cross. She stood at the foot of the cross and heard her Son promise heaven to a thief and forgive His enemies. His last words are centered on His mother and are directed to us, *Behold Thy Mother!* Let us resolve always to look upon Mary as our Mother and remember that she never fails her children.

SIXTH SORROW: *Mary Received the Body of Jesus in her Arms*

Ponder the bitter sorrow which rent the heart of Mary when the body of her dear Jesus was lowered from the cross and placed in her arms. O mournful Mother, our hearts are softened with sorrow upon seeing such affliction.

SEVENTH SORROW: *Jesus is Placed in the Tomb*

The most tragic day in history ends, and all that is left for the Mother is to accompany her Son's Body to the grave. What grief was hers as she gazed a last time on the lifeless body of her Son, and the great stone was rolled to seal the entrance to the tomb.

Let us pray

O Mother, obtain that all our love may rest with you and your Son, Our Saviour, Who shed His blood for our salvation. By all your sorrows, grant that the memory of them may be ever imprinted on our mind, that our hearts may burn with love for God, and for the Passion of Jesus: to Him be honor, glory and thanksgiving for ever and ever. Amen.

THE WAY
OF THE
CROSS
(From the Passionist Fathers)

Prayer

Crucified Jesus, behold me at Your feet. I ask Your pardon for having wandered so often into the bypaths of sin. In making this Way of the Cross give me courage to follow faithfully in Your blood-stained path.

I STATION: *Jesus Is Condemned To Death*

Our innocent Saviour accepts the unjust sentence of death on the Cross to atone for my sins.

Petition: Divine Jesus, help me to accept the injustices of life in reparation for my many sins.

II STATION: *Jesus Carries His Cross*

The burden of the Cross demanded heroic sacrifice from our Blessed Lord, yet, willingly He accepts it for love of us.

Petition: O Lord, give me the courage to take up my Cross daily and to carry it patiently along life's way.

III STATION: *Jesus Falls The First Time*

The heavy Cross and the weight of man's sinfulness overwhelm the Divine Victim and He falls into the dust of the street.

Petition: My Jesus, when the sorrows of life overwhelm me, help me to rise above human weakness.

IV STATION: *Jesus Meets His Mother*

The heart of Mary was pierced with sorrow, when she saw her innocent Son carrying the Cross made so heavy by my sins.

Petition: Suffering Lord, impress on me how much I need the consolation and help of Your sorrowful Mother.

V STATION: *Simon Of Cyrene Helps Jesus Carry The Cross*

Our blessed Lord was so weak and tired that He permitted Simon to help Him carry the Cross.

Petition: Without Your help, O Jesus, I can never carry my cross in life alone.

VI STATION: *Veronica Wipes The Face Of Jesus*

The image of the Saviour was imprinted on the veil which the compassionate Veronica pressed to the face of Jesus.

Petition: Suffering Master, may I often think of You, that the loving memory of Your sufferings be imprinted on my heart.

VII STATION: *The Second Fall Of Jesus*

Because of agonizing pain and weakness, Jesus falls once more, but rising again, carries the Cross onward.

Petition: O Lord, by this fall strengthen me against discouragement, and help me never to stop loving and serving You.

VIII STATION: *Jesus Consoles The Women Of Jerusalem*

Jesus forgets His own sorrow and pain to console the weeping women of Jerusalem.

Petition: Blessed Saviour, in sorrows and afflictions assist me to forget myself and to help others.

IX STATION: *The Third Fall Of Jesus*

On the slopes of Calvary Jesus falls the third time, yet He struggles to His feet, determined to reach the place of sacrifice.

Petition: O Divine Master, give me courage to persevere in leading a good life and reaching heaven.

X STATION: *Jesus Is Stripped Of His Garments*

The blood-soaked garments are torn from the scourged body of Jesus, so He might die stripped of every comfort in life.

Petition: Agonizing Jesus, strip me of all intemperance in the use of life's comfort and pleasures.

XI STATION: *Jesus Is Nailed To The Cross*

How frightful the agony of Jesus as the soldiers hammer rough nails through His hands and feet.

Petition: Crucified Saviour, You forgave Your enemies, teach me to also forgive injuries and to forget them.

XII STATION: *Jesus Dies On The Cross*

The Divine Victim, obedient unto death, gives the supreme proof of His love for men.

Petition: My Jesus, help me to make my return of love by life-long obedience to Your commandments.

XIII STATION: *Jesus Is Taken Down From The Cross*

What grief and tragedy as Mary holds to her broken heart, the lifeless body of Her Son.

Petition: O Mother of Sorrows, keep close to me during life and especially at the hour of my death.

XIV STATION: *Jesus Is Laid In The Sepulcher*

The Body of Jesus was reverently laid in the tomb by His loving Mother and devoted disciples.

Petition: Dear Mother Mary, help me to make my heart a fit resting place for the Body of Jesus, when I receive Him in Holy Communion.

A COLLECTION
OF GOLDEN
PRAYERS

This section of the book contains a collection of old, and new prayers. Prayers for groups, or individuals; for everyday or special needs; in praise, and in petition.

THE SALVE REGINA

Hail, Holy Queen, Mother of Mercy.

Our life, our sweetness and our hope!

To you do we cry, poor banished children of Eve.

To you do we send up our sighs; mourning and weeping in this vale of tears.

Turn then, most gracious Advocate, your eyes of mercy toward us; and after this, our exile, show unto us the blessed fruit of your womb, Jesus.

O clement, O loving, O sweet Virgin Mary.

Pray for us, O holy Mother of God. That we may be made worthy of the promises of Christ.

THE MEMORARE

Remember, O most gracious Virgin Mary, that never was it known that anyone who fled to your protection, implored your help, or sought your intercession was left unaided.

Inspired by this confidence, I fly unto you, O Virgin of virgins, my mother. To you do I come, before you I stand, sinful and sorrowful.

O Mother of the Word Incarnate, despise not my petitions, but in your mercy, hear and answer me. Amen.

THE ANGELUS

V. The Angel of the Lord declared unto Mary,

R. And she conceived of the Holy Spirit.

Hail Mary. . .

V. Behold the handmaid of the Lord.

R. Be it done unto me according to Your Word.

Hail Mary. . .

V. And the Word was made flesh.

R. And dwelt among us.

Hail Mary. . .

V. Pray for us, O Holy Mother of God.

R. That we may be made worthy of the promises of Christ.

Let us pray: *Pour forth, we beseech Thee, O Lord, Thy Grace into our hearts, that we to whom the Incarnation of Christ, Thy Son, was made known by the message of an angel, may by His passion and cross be brought to the glory of His Resurrection, through the same Christ, our Lord.* Amen.

ACT OF CONSECRATION TO THE IMMACULATE HEART OF MARY

Queen of the Most Holy Rosary, and tender Mother of all people, I consecrate myself to you and to your Immaculate Heart, and recommend to you my family, my country, and the whole human race.

Please accept my consecration, dearest Mother, and use me as you wish, to accomplish your designs upon the world.

O Immaculate Heart of Mary, Queen of Heaven and Earth, rule over me, and teach me how to allow the heart of Jesus to rule and triumph in me and around me, as it has ruled and triumphed in you. Amen.

(Pope Pius XII asked for the renewal of the Consecration to the Immaculate Heart of Mary, every year on May 31st—ad coeli Reginam.)

PRAYERS TAUGHT TO THE CHILDREN
AT FATIMA (1917)

PARDON PRAYER *(taught by the Angel)*

O My God, I believe, I adore, I trust and I love You! And I beg pardon for those who do not believe, do not adore, do not trust, and do not love You.

PRAYER OF REPARATION *(With the Blessed Sacrament suspended in the air, the Angel at Fatima prostrated himself and recited this prayer.)*

O Most Holy Trinity, Father, Son and Holy Spirit, I adore You profoundly. I offer You the most precious Body, Blood, Soul and Divinity of Jesus Christ, present in all the tabernacles of the world, in reparation for the outrages, sacrileges and indifference by which He is offended. By the infinite merits of the Sacred Heart of Jesus and the Immaculate Heart of Mary, I beg the conversion of poor sinners.

EUCHARISTIC PRAYER

Most Holy Trinity, I adore You! My God, my God, I love You in the Most Blessed Sacrament!

SACRIFICE PRAYER *(to be said in offering to Our Lord our pains and hurts, both physically and mentally, in reparation.)*

O my Jesus, it is for love of You, in reparation for the offenses committed against the Immaculate Heart of Mary, and for the conversion of poor sinners.

ROSARY DECADE PRAYER *(to be said at the end of each decade of the Rosary.)*

O my Jesus, forgive us our sins, save us from the fires of hell. Lead all souls to Heaven, especially those most in need of Your mercy.

PRAYER TO THE
SACRED HEART OF JESUS

O most Sacred Heart of Jesus, fountain of every blessing, I adore You, I love You and with true sorrow for
my sins, I offer You this poor heart of mine. Make me
humble, patient, pure and wholly obedient to Your will.
Grant, good Jesus, that I may live in You and for You.

Protect me in the midst of danger, comfort me in my
afflictions, give me health of body, assistance in my tem-
poral needs, Your blessing on all that I do, and the grace
of a holy death. Amen.

INDULGENCED
EJACULATIONS

Merciful Jesus, I consecrate myself today and always
to Your Most Sacred Heart.

Most Sacred Heart of Jesus, I implore that I may ever
love You more and more.

Most Sacred Heart of Jesus, I trust in You!

Most Sacred Heart of Jesus, have mercy on me!

Sacred Heart of Jesus, I believe in Your love for me.

Jesus, meek and humble of heart, make my heart like
Your heart.

ACT OF CONSECRATION
TO THE SACRED HEART OF JESUS

O Sacred Heart of Jesus, filled with infinite love, broken by my ingratitude, pierced by my sins, yet loving me
still—accept the consecration that I make to You of all
that I am and all that I have. Take every faculty of my
soul and body. Draw me, day by day, nearer and nearer
to your Sacred Heart, and there, as I can bear the lesson,
teach me Your blessed ways. Amen.

PRAYER TO THE HOLY SPIRIT

Oh, Holy Spirit, beloved of my soul . . . I adore You. Enlighten me, guide me, strengthen me, console me. Tell me what I should do . . . give me Your orders. I promise to submit myself to all that You desire of me and to accept all that You permit to happen to me. Let me only know Your will.

(This submission to the Holy Spirit is the Secret of Sanctity— Cardinal Mercier.)

PRAYER FOR THE SEVEN GIFTS OF THE HOLY SPIRIT

O Lord Jesus Christ, Who, before ascending into heaven, did promise to send the Holy Spirit to finish Your work in the souls of Your Apostles and Disciples—deign to grant the same Holy Spirit to me, to perfect in my soul the work of Your grace and Your love.

Grant me the Spirit of Wisdom—that I may not be attached to the perishable things of this world, but aspire only after the things that are eternal.

The Spirit of Understanding—to enlighten my mind with the light of Your divine truth.

The Spirit of Counsel—that I may ever choose the surest way of pleasing God and gaining heaven.

The Spirit of Fortitude—that I may bear my cross with You, and that I may overcome with courage all the obstacles that oppose my salvation.

The Spirit of Knowledge—that I may know God and know myself, and grow perfect in the science of the Saints.

The Spirit of Piety—that I may find the service of God sweet and amiable.

The Spirit of Fear—that I may be filled with a loving reverence towards God and may avoid anything that may displease Him.

Mark me, dear Lord, with the sign of Your true disciples, and animate me in all things with Your Spirit. Amen.

MORNING PRAYER
TO THE HOLY SPIRIT

Come, Holy Spirit, fill my heart with Your holy gifts.

Let my weakness be penetrated with Your strength this very day that I may fulfill all the duties of my state conscientiously, that I may do what is right and just.

Let my charity be such as to offend no one, and hurt no one's feelings; so generous as to pardon sincerely any wrong done to me.

Assist me, O Holy Spirit, in all my trials of life, enlighten me in my ignorance, advise me in my doubts, strengthen me in my weakness, help me in all my needs, protect me in temptations and console me in afflictions.

Graciously hear me, O Holy Spirit, and pour Your light into my heart, my soul, and my mind.

Assist me to live a holy life and to grow in goodness and grace. Amen.

MORNING OFFERING

O Jesus, through the Immaculate Heart of Mary, I offer you my prayers, works, joys and suffering of this day—for all the intentions of the Sacred Heart, in union with the Holy Sacrifice of the Mass throughout the world, in reparation for my sins, for the intentions of all my associates and for the general intention recommended this month by our Holy Father, the Pope. Amen.

MORNING THANK YOU PRAYER

I adore You, my God, and I love You with all my heart. I thank You for having created me, and for showing me Your love. Thank You for keeping me safe this night. I offer You my actions of this day; grant that they all may be according to Your holy will and for Your greater glory. Keep me from sin and all evil. May Your grace be always with me and with all my dear ones. Amen.

MAGNIFICAT

My soul magnifies the Lord,
and my spirit rejoices in God my Saviour;

Because he has regarded the lowliness of his handmaid;
for, behold, henceforth all generations shall call me blessed;

Because he who is mighty has done great things for me,
and holy is his name;

And his mercy is from generation to generation on those
who fear him.

He has shown might with his arm,
he has scattered the proud in the conceit of their heart.

He has put down the mighty from their thrones,
and has exalted the lowly.

He has filled the hungry with good things,
and the rich he has sent away empty.

He has given help to Israel, his servant, mindful of his
mercy—

Even as he spoke to our fathers—
to Abraham and to his posterity forever.

SPIRITUAL COMMUNION

*By a rescript of November 24, 1922 the Sacred Congregation of In-
dulgences approved the following formula for a spiritual communion:*

O Jesus I turn toward the holy tabernacle where You
live hidden for love of me. I love you, O my God. I
cannot receive you in Holy Communion. Come neverthe-
less and visit me with Your grace. Come spiritually into
my heart. Purify it. Sanctify it. Render it like unto Your
own. Amen.

Lord, I am not worthy that thou shouldst enter under
my roof, but only say the word and my soul shall be healed.

GUARDIAN ANGEL PRAYER

Angel of God, my guardian dear, to whom God's love
commits me here; ever this day be at my side, to light
and guard, to rule and guide. Amen.

46

LEARNING CHRIST

Teach me, my Lord, to be sweet and gentle in all the events of life, in disappointments, in the thoughtlessness of those I trusted, in the unfaithfulness of those on whom I relied. Let me put myself aside, to think of the happiness of others, to hide my little pains and heartaches, so that I may be the only one to suffer from them. Teach me to profit by the suffering that comes across my path. Let me so use it that it may mellow me, not harden nor embitter me; that it may make me patient, not irritable. That it may make me broad in my forgiveness, not narrow, haughty and overbearing. May no one be less good for having come within my influence. No one less pure, less true, less kind, less noble for having been a fellow-traveler in our journey toward Eternal Life. As I go my rounds from one distraction to another, let me whisper from time to time, a word of love to Thee. May my life be lived in the supernatural, full of power for good, and strong in its purpose of sanctity. Amen.

PRAYER FOR FAITH

Lord, I believe; I wish to believe in Thee.

Lord, let my faith be full and unreserved, and let it penetrate my thought, my way of judging Divine things and human things.

Lord, let my faith be joyful and give peace and gladness to my spirit, and dispose it for prayer with God and conversation with men, so that the inner bliss of its fortunate possession may shine forth in sacred and secular conversation.

Lord, let my faith be humble and not presume to be based on the experience of my thought and of my feeling; but let it surrender to the testimony of the Holy Spirit, and not have any better guarantee than in docility to Tradition and to the authority of the magisterium of Holy Church. Amen.   *(Pope Paul VI)*

PRAYER BEFORE CONFESSION

Come Holy Spirit into my soul.

Enlighten my mind that I may know the sins I ought to confess, and grant me Your grace to confess them fully, humbly and with contrite heart.

Help me to firmly resolve not to commit them again.

O Blessed Virgin, Mother of my Redeemer, mirror of innocence and sanctity, and refuge of penitent sinners, intercede for me through the Passion of Your Son, that I may obtain the grace to make a good confession.

All you blessed Angels and Saints of God, pray for me, a most miserable sinner, that I may repent from my evil ways, that my heart may henceforth be forever united with yours in eternal love. Amen.

ACT OF CONTRITION

O my God, I am heartily sorry for having offended You. I detest all my sins because I dread the loss of heaven and the pains of hell.

But most of all because they offend You, my God, Who are all good and deserving of all my love.

I firmly resolve, with the help of Your grace to sin no more and to avoid the near occasions of sin. Amen.

PRAYER AFTER CONFESSION

My dearest Jesus, I have told all my sins to the best of my ability. I have sincerely tried to make a good confession and I know that You have forgiven me. Thank You dear Jesus! Your divine heart is full of love and mercy for poor sinners. I love You dear Jesus; You are so good to me. My loving Saviour, I shall try to keep from sin and to love You more each day.

Dearest Mother Mary, pray for me and help me to keep all of my promises. Protect me and do not let me fall back into sin.

Dear God, help me to lead a good life. Without Your grace I can do nothing. Amen.

PRAYER BEFORE HOLY COMMUNION

Almighty and Eternal God, behold I come to the Sacrament of Your only-begotten Son, our Lord Jesus Christ. As one sick, I come to the Physician of life; unclean, to the Fountain of mercy; blind, to the Light of eternal splendor; poor and needy, to the Lord of heaven and earth. Therefore, I beg of You, through Your infinite mercy and generosity, heal my weakness, wash my uncleanness, give light to my blindness, enrich my poverty, and clothe my nakedness. May I thus receive the Bread of Angels, the King of Kings, the Lord of Lords, with such reverence and humility, contrition and devotion, purity and faith, purpose and intention, as shall aid my soul's salvation.

Grant, I beg of You, that I may receive not only the Sacrament of the Body and Blood of our Lord, but also its full grace and power. Give me the grace, most merciful God, to receive the Body of Your only Son, our Lord Jesus Christ born of the Virgin Mary, in such a manner that I may deserve to be intimately united with His mystical Body and to be numbered among His members.

Most loving Father, grant that I may behold for all eternity face to face Your beloved Son, whom now, on my pilgrimage, I am about to receive under the sacramental veil, who lives and reigns with You, in the unity of the Holy Spirit, God, world without end. Amen.

(St. Thomas Aquinas)

PRAYER BEFORE HOLY COMMUNION

Come, O blessed Saviour, and nourish my soul with heavenly Food, the Food which contains every sweetness and every delight. Come, Bread of Angels, and satisfy the hunger of my soul. Come, glowing Furnace of Charity, and enkindle in my heart the flame of divine love. Come, Light of the World, and enlighten the darkness of my mind. Come, King of Kings, and make me obedient to Your holy will. Come, loving Saviour, and make me meek and humble. Come, Friend of the Sick, and heal the infirmities of my body and the weakness of my soul. Come, Good Shepherd, my God and my All, and take me to Yourself.

O most holy Mother, Mary Immaculate, prepare my heart to receive my Saviour.

PRAYER AFTER HOLY COMMUNION

Praise be to You, O Lord, who fill heaven and earth with Your Majesty, and yet You have been pleased to nourish me with this most holy Sacrament. Cleanse me, my God, from every stain of soul and body, and teach me to walk in Your fear and do good, so that my conscience may prove that I have been sanctified by the receiving of Your holy Body and Blood, and that my soul is indeed a temple of the Holy Spirit. Merciful Lord, let me not increase my guilt through an unworthy reception of this Sacrament, but grant that it may be a means of making me more pleasing to You.

Father of mercy and God of all consolation, graciously look upon me and impart to me the blessing which flows from this holy Sacrament. Overshadow me with Your loving kindness, and let this divine Mystery bear fruit in me.

I thank you, Almighty and Merciful Father. I am deeply grateful to You for having had pity on me and cleansed me from sin and allowed me to have a share in this Sacrament on which the angels desire to gaze. Grant that this sacred union with You may bring me pardon for my past sins, a remedy for those which I may still have, and a safeguard against those I might commit in the future, who live and reign as God forever. Amen.

(St. Blase)

ACT OF THANKSGIVING

From the depths of my heart I thank You, dear Lord, for Your infinite kindness in coming to me. How good You are to me! With Your most holy Mother and all the angels, I praise Your mercy and generosity toward me, a poor sinner. I thank You for nourishing my soul with Your Sacred Body and Precious Blood. I will try to show my gratitude to You in the Sacrament of Your love, by obedience to Your holy commandments, by fidelity to my duties, by kindness to my neighbor and by an earnest endeavor to become more like You in my daily conduct.

Grant that I may spend the hours of the day gladly working with You according to Your will.

Help me just for today and be with me in it. In the long hours of work, that I may not grow weary or slack in serving You.

In conversations, that they may not be to me occasions of uncharitableness.

In the day's worries and disappointments, that I may be patient with myself and with those around me.

In moments of fatigue and illness, that I may be mindful of others rather than of myself.

In temptations, that I may be generous and loyal, so that when the day is over I may lay it at Your feet, with its successes which are all Yours, and its failures which are all my own, and feel that life is real and peaceful, and blessed when spent with You as the Guest of my soul. Amen.

Lord, I give thanks to You for Your dying
on the Cross for my sins.

PRAYER BEFORE A CRUCIFIX

Look down upon me, O Good and Gentle Jesus, while before Your face I humbly kneel, and with the most fervent desire of my soul, I pray and beseech You to fix deep in my heart lively sentiments of faith, hope and charity, true contrition for my sins, and a firm purpose of amendment; while with deep affection and grief of soul I mentally contemplate Your five most precious wounds, recalling to mind the words which David, Your prophet, said concerning You: *They have pierced My hands and My feet, they have numbered all My bones.*

ACT OF ADORATION

Jesus, my God, I adore You, here present in the Blessed Sacrament of the altar, where You wait day and night to be our comfort while we await Your unveiled presence in heaven. Jesus, my God, I adore You in all places where the Blessed Sacrament is reserved, in reparation for sins committed against this Sacrament of Love. Jesus, my God, I adore You for all time, past, present and future, for every soul that ever was, is or shall be created. Jesus, my God, who for us has endured hunger and cold, labor and fatigue, I adore You. Jesus, my God, who for my sake has deigned to subject Yourself to the humiliation of temptation, to the perfidy and defection of friends, to the scorn of Your enemies, I adore You. Jesus, my God, who for us has endured the buffeting of Your passion, the scourging, the crowning with thorns, the heavy weight of the Cross, I adore You. Jesus, my God, who, for my salvation and that of all mankind, was cruelly nailed to the Cross and hung there for three long hours in bitter agony, I adore You. Jesus, my God, who for love of us did institute this Blessed Sacrament and offer Yourself daily for the sins of men, I adore You. Jesus, my God, who in Holy Communion became the food of my soul, I adore You.

Jesus, for You I live. Jesus, for You I die. Jesus, I am Yours in life and death. *(John J. Cardinal Carberry)*

AN ACT OF FAITH

O my God, I firmly believe that You are one God in three Divine Persons, Father, Son, and Holy Spirit; I believe that Your Divine Son became man and died for our sins, and that He will come to judge the living and the dead. I believe these and all the truths which the Holy Catholic Church teaches, because You revealed them, who can neither deceive nor be deceived.

(Partial indulgence)

AN ACT OF HOPE

O my God, relying on Your infinite goodness and promises, I hope to obtain pardon of my sins, the help of Your grace, and life everlasting, through the merits of Jesus Christ, my Lord and Redeemer.

(Partial indulgence)

AN ACT OF LOVE

O my God, I love You above all things, with my whole heart and soul, because You are all-good and worthy of all love. I love my neighbor as myself for the love of You. I forgive all who have injured me, and I ask pardon of all whom I have injured. *(Partial indulgence)*

Lord Jesus Christ, Son of the Living God,
Have mercy on me, a sinner.

THE CHAPLET OF MERCY
(To be said on regular rosary beads.)

Begin by saying one each:

Our Father. . . Hail Mary. . . The Creed...

On the large beads say:

Eternal Father, I offer You the Body and Blood, Soul and Divinity of Your dearly beloved Son, Our Lord Jesus Christ, in atonement for our sins and those of the whole world.

On the small beads say:

For the sake of His sorrowful Passion, have mercy on us and on the whole world.

Repeat the above for every decade of the rosary. In conclusion say:

Holy God, Holy Mighty One, Holy Immortal One, have mercy on us and on the whole world. (3 times.)

(With Ecclesiastical Permission)

A PRAYER FOR DIVINE MERCY

O Great Merciful God, Infinite Goodness, today all mankind calls out from the abyss of its misery to Your mercy— to Your compassion, O God; and it is with its mighty voice of misery that it cries out. Gracious God, do not reject the prayer of this earth's exiles! O Lord, Goodness beyond our understanding, Who are acquainted with our misery through and through, and know that by our own power we cannot ascend to You, we implore You, anticipate us with Your grace and keep on increasing Your mercy in us, that we may faithfully do Your holy will all through our life and at death's hour. Let the omnipotence of Your mercy shield us from the darts of our salvation's enemies, that we may with confidence, as Your children, await Your final coming—that day known to You alone. And we expect to obtain everything promised us by Jesus in spite of all our wretchedness, for Jesus is our Hope. Through His merciful Heart, as through an open gate, we pass through to heaven.

(From the Diary of the Servant of God, by Sr. Faustina)
Imprimatur: J. F. Maguire, Bishop of Springfield, MA. Nov. 13, 1979.

54

PRAYER FOR PEACE

O God, from Whom proceeds all holy desires, all right counsels and all just works; grant unto us Your servants that peace which the world cannot give. May our hearts be devoted to Your service, and that, being delivered from the fear of our enemies, we may pass our time in peace under Your protection. Through Christ Our Lord, Amen.

PRAYER TO ST. MICHAEL

St. Michael the Archangel, defend us in the day of Battle; Be our safeguard against the wickedness and snares of the Devil. May God rebuke him, we humbly pray, and do Thou, O Prince of the Heavenly Host, by the power of God, cast into Hell, Satan and all the other evil spirits, who prowl through the world, seeking the ruin of souls. Amen.

(This powerful prayer of exorcism was composed by Pope Leo XIII; in a vision, he had been shown the fearful battle to be waged between Satan and St. Michael, over the Church of the future. Now, as never before, the Church needs the intercession of St. Michael! Please say this prayer every day.)

PRAYER TO DEFEAT THE WORK OF SATAN

O Divine Eternal Father, in union with your Divine Son and the Holy Spirit, and through the Immaculate Heart of Mary, I beg You to destroy the Power of your greatest enemy—the evil spirits.

Cast them into the deepest recesses of hell and chain them there forever! Take possession of your Kingdom which You have created and which is rightfully yours.

Heavenly Father, give us the reign of the Sacred Heart of Jesus and the Immaculate Heart of Mary.

I repeat this prayer out of pure love for You with every beat of my heart and with every breath I take. Amen.

Imprimatur: ✠ Richard H. Ackerman
                      Bishop of Covington

March 1973

TO ST. MONICA, PATRONESS OF MOTHERS

Blessed Monica, mother of St. Augustine, we give thanks to our Father in heaven who looked with mercy upon your tears over your wayward son. His conversion and heroic sanctification were the fruit of your prayers. Dear St. Monica we now ask you to pray with us for all those sons and daughters that have wandered away from God, and to add your prayers to those of all mothers who are worried over their children. Pray also for us that, following your example, we may, in the company of our children, one day enjoy the eternal vision of our Father in heaven. Amen.

PARENTS PRAYER TO THE HOLY FAMILY

Jesus, Son of the Eternal Father, we most fervently implore You to take our children under Your special care and enclose them in the love of Your Sacred Heart. Rule and guide them that they may live according to our holy Faith, that they may not waiver in their confidence in You, and may ever remain faithful in Your love.

O Mary, blessed Mother of Jesus, grant to our children a place in your pure maternal heart. Spread over them your protecting mantle when danger threatens their innocence; keep them firm when they are tempted to stray from the path of virtue; and should they have the misfortune to fall, oh, raise them up again and reconcile them with your Divine Son.

Holy foster father, St. Joseph, watch over our children. Protect them from the assaults of the wicked enemy, and deliver them from all dangers of soul and body.

Mary and Joseph, dear parents of the holy Child Jesus, intercede for us that we may be a good example and bring up our children in the love and fear of God, and one day attain with them the Beatific Vision in Heaven. Amen.

PRAYER FOR A FAMILY

O dear Jesus, I humbly implore You to grant Your special graces to our family. May our home be the shrine of peace, purity, love, labor and faith. I beg You, dear Jesus, to protect and bless all of us, absent and present, living and dead.

O Mary, loving Mother of Jesus, and our Mother, pray to Jesus for our family, for all the families of the world, to guard the cradle of the newborn, the schools of the young and their vocations.

Blessed Saint Joseph, holy guardian of Jesus and Mary, assist us by your prayers in all the necessities of life. Ask of Jesus that special grace which He granted to you, to watch over our home at the pillow of the sick and the dying, so that with Mary and with you, heaven may find our family unbroken in the Sacred Heart of Jesus. Amen.

PRAYER OF SPOUSES FOR EACH OTHER

Lord Jesus, grant that I and my spouse may have a true and understanding love for each other. Grant that we may both be filled with faith and trust. Give us the grace to live with each other in peace and harmony. May we always bear with one another's weaknesses and grow from each other's strengths. Help us to forgive one another's failings and grant us patience, kindness, cheerfulness and the spirit of placing the well-being of one another ahead of self.

May the love that brought us together grow and mature with each passing year. Bring us both ever closer to You through our love for each other. Let our love grow to perfection. Amen.

PRAYER FOR THE
SOULS IN PURGATORY

O gentle Heart of Jesus, ever present in the Blessed Sacrament, ever consumed with burning love for the poor captive souls in Purgatory, have mercy on them.

Let some drops of Your Precious Blood fall upon the devouring flames. And, Merciful Saviour, send Your angels to conduct them to a place of refreshment, light and peace. Amen.

Eternal rest grant unto them, O Lord, and let perpetual light shine upon them.

May the souls of the faithful departed, through the mercy of God, rest in peace. Amen.

FOR A HOLY DEATH

O my Lord and Saviour, support me in my last hour by the strong arms of Your Sacraments and by the power of Your consolations.

Let the absolving words be said over me, and the holy oil sign and seal me.

Let Your own body and blood be my food and drink; and let my Mother, Mary, breathe on me and my angel whisper peace to me.

May the glorious saints and my own patrons smile upon me that, in them all and through them all, I may receive the gift of perseverance, and die as I desire to live in Your Church, in Your service, and in Your love. Amen.

(Cardinal Newman)

PRAYER FOR THE DYING

Most Merciful Jesus, lover of souls, I pray You, by the agony of Your most Sacred Heart, and by the sorrows of Your Immaculate Mother, to wash in Your Most Precious Blood, the sinners of the world who are now in their agony, and who will die today.

Heart of Jesus, once in agony, have mercy on the dying. Amen.

PRAYER TO ST. JOSEPH
FOR A HAPPY DEATH

O Powerful, St. Joseph, great patron of the dying, you who breathed your last in the arms of Jesus and Mary, I implore you to stand by me at the hour of my death. Remember at that time, how often I have called upon you. Obtain for me perfect contrition for my sins, firm confidence in the mercy of God, firm trust in the merits of my Saviour and the grace to breathe forth my soul while sweetly calling upon the holy names, Jesus, Mary and Joseph. Obtain this favor for me through your Divine Foster Son, Jesus Christ, Who with the Father and the Holy Spirit lives and reigns forever and ever. Amen.

Jesus, Mary and Joseph, I give you my heart and my soul!

Jesus, Mary and Joseph, assist me in my last agony.

Jesus, Mary and Joseph, may I breathe forth my soul at peace in your blessed company!

PRAYER FOR THE POOR SOULS
(Taught to St. Gertrude)

(Our Lord told St. Gertrude the Great that the following prayer would release a vast number of souls from Purgatory each time it is said.)

Eternal Father, I offer Thee the most Precious Blood of Thy Divine Son, Jesus, in union with all the Masses being said this day throughout the world for all the holy souls in Purgatory. Amen.

(Approval of His Emminence the Cardinal Patriarch of Lisbon—4/3/1936.)

FOR THE POOR

Make us worthy, Lord, to serve those people throughout the world who live and die in poverty and hunger. Give them through our hands, this day, their daily bread, and by our understanding love, give them peace and joy.

(Mother Teresa of Calcutta)

A PRAYER OF
ST. ALPHONSUS LIGUORI
FOR FIVE GRACES

Eternal Father, Your Son has promised that You would grant all the graces we ask of You in His name. Trusting in this promise, and in the name and through the merits of Jesus Christ, I ask of You five graces:

First, I ask pardon for all offenses I have committed, for which I am sorry with all my heart, because I have offended Your infinite goodness.

Second, I ask for Your divine Light, which will enable me to see the vanity of all the things of this earth, and see also Your infinite greatness and goodness.

Third, I ask for a share in Your love, so that I can detach myself from all creatures, especially from myself, and love only Your holy will.

Fourth, grant me the grace to have confidence in the merits of Jesus Christ and in the intercession of Mary.

Fifth, I ask for the grace of perseverance, knowing that whenever I call on You for assistance, You will answer my call and come to my aid; I fear only that I will neglect to turn to You in time of need, and thus bring myself to ruin.

Grant me the grace to pray always, O Eternal Father, in the name of Jesus. Amen.

PRAYER OF DAILY NEGLECTS

Eternal Father, I offer You the Sacred Heart of Jesus, with all its Love, all its Sufferings and all its Merits.

To expiate all the sins I have committed this day and during all my life—**Glory be to the Father**...

To purify the good I have done in my poor way this day and during all my life—**Glory be to the Father**...

To make up for the good I ought to have done, and that I have neglected this day and during all my life—**Glory be to the Father**...

PRAYER FOR FORGIVENESS

Behold, O my God, the traitor who has so often rebelled against You. Alas! I am filled with regret; I abhor and detest with all my heart my innumerable sins. I offer You in expiation the same satisfaction which Jesus Christ offers on the altar; His merits, His Blood, and Himself, God Incarnate, Who, as Victim, deigns to renew His Sacrifice daily on our altars for our sake. As my Jesus is Himself my Mediator and Advocate on the altar, and is asking you to have mercy on me through His Precious Blood, I join my voice to His adorable pleading, and ask Your forgiveness for the enormity of my sins. O God of my heart, if my tears do not touch You, listen to the groanings of Jesus, and as He obtained mercy on the Cross for the whole world, may He obtain it for me on the altar! I humbly trust that through the merits of His Precious Blood You will forgive me all my sins, which I shall bewail to my last breath. My beloved Jesus, give me the tears of St. Peter, the contrition of Mary Magdalen, and the sorrow of all the Saints, who from sinners became true penitents, that I may obtain complete forgiveness of my sins through the Holy Sacrifice of the Mass. Amen.

PRAYER TO ST. DISMAS

O great Saint Dismas, whose unutterable privilege it was to die by the side of Christ expiring on the Cross, obtain for us the grace of being sorry for our sins so that we, too, at the last hour, may hear the words Our Lord spoke to you: "Amen, I say to you, this day you shall be with Me in Paradise!"

(Fr. Thomas Davitt, SJ)

61

FOR HOLY CHURCH AND FOR PRIESTS

O my Jesus, I beg You on behalf of the whole Church: Grant it love and the light of Your Spirit and give power to the words of priests so that hardened hearts might be brought to repentance and return to You, O Lord.

Lord, give us holy priests; You yourself maintain them in holiness. O Divine and Great High Priest, may the power of Your mercy accompany them everywhere and protect them from the devil's traps and snares which are continually being set for the souls of priests. May the power of Your mercy, O Lord, shatter and bring to naught all that might tarnish the sanctity of priests, for You can do all things. I ask You, Jesus, for a special blessing and for light for the priests before whom I will make my confessions throughout my lifetime. Amen.

FOR PRIESTS

Almighty God, look upon the face of Him who is the eternal High Priest, and have compassion on Your priests in today's world. Remember that they are but weak and frail human beings. Stir up in them the grace of their vocation. Keep them close to You lest the enemy prevail against them, so that they may never do anything in the slightest degree unworthy of their sublime vocation.

O Jesus, I pray for Your faithful and fervent priests, for the unfaithful and tepid ones; for those laboring at home and abroad in distant mission fields; for those who are tempted; for those who are lonely and desolate; for those who are young; for those who are dying; and for those who are in purgatory.

But, above all, I recommend to You the priests dearest to me; the priest who baptized me; the priests who absolved me from my sins; the priests at whose Masses I have assisted and who gave me Your body and blood in Holy Communion; the priests who instructed me or helped me by their encouragement. I pray devoutly for all the priests to whom I am indebted in any other way, in particular for... O Jesus, keep them all close to Your heart and bless them abundantly in time and in eternity. Amen.

O Mary, Queen of the Clergy, pray for us; obtain for us many and holy priests.

PRAYER FOR VOCATIONS

Lord, You told us that "The harvest indeed is great but the laborers are few. Pray, therefore, the Lord of the harvest to send laborers into His harvest." We ask You to strengthen us as we follow the vocation to which You have called us. We pray particularly for those called to serve as priests, sisters, brothers and deacons:

> Those whom You have called,
> Those You are calling now,
> Those You will call in the future.

May they be open and responsive to the call of serving Your people. We ask this through Christ, our Lord, Amen.

PRAYER FOR THE POPE

Lord, source of eternal life and truth, give to Your shepherd, the Pope, a spirit of courage and right judgment, a spirit of knowledge and love.

By governing with fidelity those entrusted to his care may he, as successor to the apostle Peter and vicar of Christ, build Your Church into a sacrament of unity, love, and peace for all the world.

We ask this through our Lord Jesus Christ, Your Son, Who lives and reigns with You and the Holy Spirit, one God, forever and ever. Amen.

PRAYER IN TIME OF SUFFERING

Behold me, my beloved Jesus, weighed down under the burden of my trials and sufferings, I cast myself at Your feet, that You may renew my strength and my courage, while I rest here in Your presence. Permit me to lay down my cross in Your sacred Heart, for only Your infinite goodness can sustain me; only Your love can help me bear my cross; only Your powerful hand can lighten its weight. O Divine King Jesus, whose heart is so compassionate to the afflicted, I wish to live in You; suffer and die in You. During my life, be to me my model and my support; at the hour of my death, be my hope and my refuge. Amen.

LOVE OF THE CROSS

In the Cross is salvation, in the Cross is life, in the Cross is protection against our enemies, in the Cross is infusion of heavenly sweetness, in the Cross is strength of mind, in the Cross is joy of spirit, in the Cross the height of virtue, in the Cross the perfection of holiness. There is no salvation of the soul, nor hope of everlasting life, but in the Cross. Take up therefore thy Cross and follow Jesus, and thou shalt go into everlasting life. He went before, bearing His Cross, and died for thee on the Cross; that thou also might bear thy Cross and desire to die on the Cross. For if thou be dead with Him, thou shall also in like manner live with Him. And if thou share His punishment, thou shall also share His glory. Behold! in the Cross all does consist, and in our dying, all dwell; for there is no other way unto life, and unto true inward peace, but the way of the holy Cross, and of daily mortification.
(*Thomas A. Kempis, from THE IMITATION OF CHRIST.*)

PRAYER OF THANKSGIVING

I thank You, Jesus:

For the gift of life, and every moment I live! For my health, even though at times I may have been ill, or suffered serious reverses and sufferings. So often these and other crosses are blessings in disguise. For the world about me, such as, the glories of nature, the moon, the stars, the flowers of the fields, the fruits of the earth, the very air I breathe, the refreshing rains, the glorious sunshine, the seasons of the year. For my parents, my relatives, my treasured and trusted friends.

I thank You:

For the gift of my faith. For the gift of Yourself in the Incarnation in which You became man, lived for me, taught me by Your word and example. For the gift of redemption, which You accomplished by Your sufferings, death and resurrection—all this for my salvation.

O my God, I thank You for all the favors You have bestowed upon me. I give You thanks from the bottom of my heart for having created me, and for all the joys of life, and its sorrows, too, for the home You gave me, for the loved ones with which You have surrounded me, for the friends I have made through life.

My Lord, I thank You for guarding me always and keeping me safe; I thank You for giving me so often in the sacrament of Penance forgiveness for my sins; for offering Yourself in Holy Mass with all Your infinite merits to the Father for me; for coming to me in Holy Communion, in spite of the coldness of my welcome; for the patient waiting in the adorable sacrament of the altar.

My Jesus, I thank You for having lived, suffered and died for me. I thank You for Your love. I thank You, Lord, for preparing a place for me in heaven where I hope to be happy with You, and to thank You for all eternity. Amen.

John J. Cardinal Carberry, Archbishop of St. Louis
December 8, 1977

PRAYER IN TIME OF SICKNESS

O Jesus, You suffered and died for us; You understand suffering; Teach me to understand my suffering as You do; to bear it in union with You; to offer it with You to atone for my sins and to bring Your grace to souls in need. Calm my fears; increase my trust. May I gladly accept Your holy will and become more like You in trial. If it be Your will, restore me to health so that I may work for Your honor and glory and the salvation of all mankind. Amen. Mary, help of the sick, pray for me.

A PRAYER OF MANY PRAYERS

Dear Father in Heaven, hear my prayer, and do not turn your face from those who come to you in their need. Send, now, Your Holy Spirit, to fill my mind, my heart, my soul, with the words and thoughts I want to express. Give me now, again, Your Son, the Incarnation of the Word. Give Him to me again through Your faithful handmaid, Mary, the Mother of Jesus.

Immaculate Mary, pray with me, and for me, now, and help me to be worthy of Your Son. Bring me now to Jesus. Through the gifts of Your Spouse, the Holy Spirit, help me to express my belief, my trust, my faith and my love for Your Son.

Lord Jesus, I pray in praise, in adoration, in thanksgiving that You are. I thank you for my faith, that allows me to know You exist. Help me to be more aware of Your presence, Your gifts, and blessings. Never let me forget that all that I am, all that I have comes from You. It is through Your grace, O Lord. Praise be Your name. Help me to better recognize why You came. Help me, and all Your people to see that Your presence in the world was our redemption, our salvation. Your death and resurrection was a preview of ours. You showed us victory over death, over the world, victory over Satan. Your resurrection promised us eternal life, if we are willing to take up our cross and follow You.

Lord Jesus, You are the way, the Lamb of God, the

Prince of Peace, the Good Shepherd, the Divine Healer. You brought us the sacraments, the new Church, a new covenant. Lord help us to recognize it is all Yours; that our only right is the right of choice...You, or the world.

Lord Jesus, help us to see that mankind cannot solve its own problems, just as our own conscience alone, is not enough to guide us. It cannot eliminate all the sin in our life. Our own capabilities cannot eliminate all the sin, the suffering, the pain or the violence in the world, without You. Help us to recognize the meaning of Your words: *Without Me, you can do nothing.* It is all around us, why can't we see?

Lord Jesus, help me to help Your people; Your Church, Your priests and bishops, Your brothers and sisters of all races and creeds. Help me to help them through the one means available to me...**PRAYER!**

Lord Jesus, give us all a stronger need to pray everyday. Give us an unquenchable thirst for prayer. Above all, Lord, may Your Spirit give us a greater gift of humility. Help us all to realize we do not have the power to change all the evils in the world. Only You do! Give me and all Your people, the humility to truly understand and follow Your words: *Father not my will but Thine be done.* Lord, give us the realization that submission to Your will, and answers to our needs, come only through prayer.

Lord Jesus, give us the wisdom to search for You every day in prayer, and to seek first, Your will. Amen.

FOR THE HELPLESS UNBORN

Heavenly Father, You created mankind in Your own image and You desire that not even the least among us should perish. In Your love for us, You entrusted Your only Son to the holy Virgin Mary. Now, in Your love, protect against the wickedness of the evil, those little ones to whom You have given the gift of life.

PETITIONS FROM THE SAINTS

Holy Mary, help the miserable, strengthen the discouraged, comfort the sorrowful, pray for your people, plead for the clergy, intercede for all women consecrated to God. May all who venerate you, feel now your help and protection. Be ready to help us when we pray, and bring to us the answers to our prayers. Make it your continual care to pray for the people of God, for you were blessed by God and were made worthy to bear the Redeemer of the world, Who lives and reigns forever.

(St. Augustine)

Come O Holy Spirit! Come to sanctify, to enlighten and to move our souls by Your grace, Your virtues and gifts! You are the soul of the Mystical Body of Christ. Give to the Church an ever abundant supernatural life by Your ever-present help. By Your gifts guide her infallibly in the way of truth and holiness. O uncreated Love of the Blessed Trinity, bring about among us her members, the marvellous unity which Christ has asked of the Father for us: *That they all be one, as You, Father, in Me and I in You.* *(St. Ignatius)*

Pray to and invoke the Holy Spirit; for each one of us greatly needs His protection and His help. The more a man is deficient in wisdom, weak in strength, borne down with trouble, prone to sin, the more he ought to fly to Him Who is the never-ceasing fount of light, strength, consolation, and holiness.

All preachers and those having the care of souls should remember that it is their duty to instruct their people more diligently and more fully about the Holy Spirit. What should be chiefly dwelt upon and clearly explained is the multitude and greatness of the benefits which have been bestowed, and are constantly bestowed upon us by this Divine Giver. *(Pope Leo XIII, 1897)*

O Holy Mother of God, pray for the priests Your Son has chosen to serve the Church. Help them by your intercession, to be holy, zealous and chaste. Make them models of virtue in the service of God's people.

Help them be pious in meditation, efficacious in preaching and zealous in the daily offering of the Holy Sacrifice of the Mass. Help them administer the Sacraments with joy. Amen. *(St. Charles Borromero)*

Fortify me with the grace of Your Holy Spirit and give Your peace to my soul that I may be free from all needless anxiety, solicitude and worry. Help me to desire always that which is pleasing and acceptable to you so that Your will may be my will.

Grant that I may rid myself of all unholy desires and that, for Your love, I may remain obscure and unknown in this world, to be known only to You. Do not permit me to attribute to myself the good that you perform in me and through me, but rather, referring all honor to Your Majesty, may I glory only in my infirmities, so that renouncing sincerely all vainglory which comes from the world, I may aspire to that true and lasting glory which comes from You. Amen. *(St. Frances Xavier Cabrini)*

O Heart of love, I put all my trust in You; for I fear all things from my own weakness, but I hope for all things from Your goodness.

(St. Margaret Mary Alacoque)

O Mary, powerful Virgin, you are the mighty and glorious protector of the Church; you are the marvelous help of Christians; you are powerful as an army set in battle array; you alone have destroyed every heresy in the whole world.

In the midst of our anguish, our struggles and our distress, defend us from the power of the enemy and at the hour of our death receive our souls in paradise. Amen.

(St. John Bosco)

Lord, grant that I may always allow myself to be guided by you, always follow Your plans and perfectly accomplish Your holy will.

Grant that in all things, great and small, today and all the days of my life, I may do whatever You require of me. Help me respond to the slightest prompting of Your grace so that I may be Your trustworthy instrument for Your honor.

May Your will be done in time and in eternity—by me, in me and through me. Amen.

(St. Teresa of Avila)

O Jesus, supreme master of all hearts, I love You, I adore you, I praise You, I thank You, because I am now all Yours. Rule over me and transform my soul into the likeness of Yourself, so that it may bless and glorify You forever in the abode of the saints. Amen.

(St. Margaret Mary Alacoque)

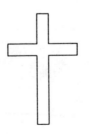

Virgin full of goodness, Mother of mercy, I entrust to you my body and soul, my thoughts, my actions, my life and my death.

O my Queen, help me, and deliver me from all the snares of the devil. Obtain for me the grace of loving my Lord Jesus Christ, your Son, with a true and perfect love, and after Him, O Mary, to love you with all my heart and above all things. *(St. Bonaventure)*

Dearest Lord, teach me to be generous; teach me to serve You as You deserve; to give and not to count the cost, to fight and not to heed the wounds, to toil and not to seek for rest, to labor and not to ask for reward except that of knowing I am doing Your will.

(St. Ignatius Loyola)

Lord, make me an instrument of Thy peace; where there is hatred, let me sow love; where there is injury, pardon; where there is doubt, faith; where there is despair, hope; where there is darkness, light; and where there is sadness, joy.

O Divine Master, grant that I may not so much seek to be consoled as to console; to be understood as to understand; to be loved, as to love; for it is in giving that we receive, it is in pardoning that we are pardoned, and it is in dying that we are born to eternal life.

(St. Francis of Assisi)

LITANY OF THE
MOST SACRED HEART OF JESUS

Lord, have mercy on us.

Christ, have mercy on us.

Lord, have mercy on us. Christ hear us.

Christ, graciously hear us.

God the Father of Heaven,

Have mercy on us.

God the Son, Redeemer of the world,

Have mercy on us.

God the Holy Spirit

Have mercy on us.

Holy Trinity, One God,

Have mercy on us.

Heart of Jesus, Son of the Eternal Father,

(Have mercy on us.)

Heart of Jesus, formed by the Holy Spirit in the womb
of the Virgin Mother,

(Have mercy on us.)

Heart of Jesus, substantially united to the Word of
God, *(etc.)*

Heart of Jesus, of infinite majesty,

Heart of Jesus, holy Temple of God,

Heart of Jesus, Tabernacle of the Most High,

Heart of Jesus, House of God and
Gate of Heaven,

Heart of Jesus, burning Furnace of charity,

Heart of Jesus, Vessel of justice and love,

Heart of Jesus, full of goodness and love,

Heart of Jesus, Abyss of all virtues,

Heart of Jesus, most worthy of all praise,

Heart of Jesus, King and center of all hearts

Heart of Jesus, in Whom are all the treasures of
wisdom and knowledge,

Heart of Jesus, in Whom dwelleth all the
fullness of the divinity,

Heart of Jesus, in Whom the Father
   was well pleased,
Heart of Jesus, of whose fullness we have
   all received
Heart of Jesus, desire of the everlasting hills,
Heart of Jesus, patient and abounding in mercy,
Heart of Jesus, rich unto all who call upon Thee,
Heart of Jesus, Fountain of life and holiness
Heart of Jesus, Propitiation for our sins,
Heart of Jesus, filled with reproaches,
Heart of Jesus, bruised for our offenses,
Heart of Jesus, obedient unto death,
Heart of Jesus, pierced with a lance,
Heart of Jesus, Source of all consolation,
Heart of Jesus, our Life and Resurrection,
Heart of Jesus, our Peace and Reconciliation,
Heart of Jesus, Victim for our sins,
Heart of Jesus, Salvation of those who hope in Thee,
Heart of Jesus, Hope of those who die in Thee,
Heart of Jesus, Delight of all the saints,

Lamb of God, Who takest away the sins of the world,
   Spare us, O Lord.
Lamb of God, Who takest away the sins of the world,
   Graciously hear us, O Lord.
Lamb of God, Who takest away the sins of the world,
   Have mercy on us.

V. Jesus meek and humble of heart,
R. *Make our hearts like unto Thine.*

Let us pray

   Almighty and eternal God, consider the Heart of Your
well-beloved Son and the praises and satisfaction He offers
You in the name of sinners; appeased by worthy homage,
pardon those who implore Your mercy, in the name of
the same Jesus Christ Your Son, Who lives and reigns with
You, world without end. Amen.

THE LITANY OF THE
BLESSED VIRGIN MARY

Lord have mercy on us.
  Christ, have mercy on us.
Lord, have mercy on us. Christ, hear us.
  Christ, graciously hear us.
God the Father of Heaven,
  Have mercy on us.
God the Son, Redeemer of the world,
  Have mercy on us.
God the Holy Spirit,
  Have mercy on us.
Holy Trinity, One God,
  Have mercy on us.

Holy Mary, *(pray for us)*.
Holy Mother of God, *(pray for us)*.
Holy Virgin of virgins, *(etc.)*.
Mother of Christ,
Mother of divine grace,
Mother most pure,
Mother most chaste,
Mother inviolate,
Mother undefiled,
Mother most amiable,
Mother most admirable,
Mother of good counsel,
Mother of our Creator,
Mother of our Saviour,
Mother of the Church,
Virgin most prudent,
Virgin most venerable,
Virgin most renowned,
Virgin most powerful,
Virgin most merciful,
Virgin most faithful,
Mirror of justice,

Seat of wisdom,
Cause of our joy,
Spiritual vessel,
Vessel of honor,
Singular vessel of devotion,
Mystical rose,
Tower of David,
Tower of ivory,
House of gold,
Ark of the covenant,
Gate of Heaven,
Morning star,
Health of the sick,
Refuge of sinners,
Comforter of the afflicted,
Help of Christians,
Queen of angels,
Queen of patriarchs,
Queen of prophets,
Queen of apostles,
Queen of martyrs,
Queen of confessors,
Queen of virgins,
Queen of all saints,
Queen conceived without Original Sin,
Queen assumed into Heaven,
Queen of the most holy Rosary,
Queen of peace,

Lamb of God, Who takest away the sins of the world,
Spare us, O Lord.
Lamb of God, Who takest away the sins of the world,
Graciously hear us, O Lord.
Lamb of God, Who takest away the sins of the world,
Have mercy on us.

V. Pray for us, O Holy Mother of God,
R. *That we may be made worthy of the promises of Christ.*

Let us pray

Grant, we beseech You, O Lord God, that we Your servants may enjoy perpetual health of mind and body, and by the glorious intercession of the Blessed Mary, ever Virgin, be delivered from present sorrow and enjoy everlasting happiness. Through Christ Our Lord. Amen.

LITANY OF ST. JOSEPH

Lord, have mercy on us.
Christ, have mercy on us.
Lord, have mercy on us. Christ, hear us.
Christ, graciously hear us.
God the Father of Heaven,
Have mercy on us.
God the Son, Redeemer of the world,
Have mercy on us.
God the Holy Ghost,
Have mercy on us.
Holy Trinity, One God
Have mercy on us.

Holy Mary, *pray for us.*
St. Joseph, *pray for us.*
Illustrious son of David, *etc.*
Light of the patriarchs,
Spouse of the Mother of God,
Chaste guardian of the Virgin,

76

Foster-father of the Son of God,
Diligent protector of Christ,
Head of the Holy Family,
Joseph most just,
Joseph most chaste,
Joseph most prudent,
Joseph most valiant,
Joseph most obedient,
Joseph most faithful,
Mirror of patience,
Lover of poverty,
Model of workers,
Glory of home life,
Guardian of virgins,
Pillar of families,
Solace of the afflicted,
Hope of the sick,
Patron of the dying,
Terror of demons,
Protector of Holy Church,

Lamb of God, Who takest away the sins of the world,
Spare us, O Lord.
Lamb of God, Who takest away the sins of the world,
Graciously hear us, O Lord.
Lamb of God, Who takest away the sins of the world,
Have mercy on us.

V. He made him the lord of His household.
R. *And prince over all His possessions.*

Let us pray

O God, Who in Your ineffable providence didst vouchsafe to choose blessed Joseph to be the spouse of Your most holy Mother; grant, we beseech You, that we may have him for our intercessor in Heaven, whom we venerate as our protector on earth: Who livest and reignest world without end. Amen.

THE
ANIMA CHRISTI
OF ST. ELIZABETH ANN SETON
(For private use only.)

Soul of Jesus,
  Sanctify me.
Blood of Jesus,
  Wash me.
Passion of Jesus,
  Comfort me.
Wounds of Jesus,
  Hide me.
Heart of Jesus,
  Receive me.
Spirit of Jesus,
  Enliven me.
Goodness of Jesus,
  Pardon me.
Beauty of Jesus,
  Draw me.
Humility of Jesus,
  Humble me.
Peace of Jesus,
  Pacify me.
Love of Jesus,
  Inflame me,
Kingdom of Jesus,
  Come to me.
Grace of Jesus,
  Replenish me.
Mercy of Jesus,
  Pity me.
Sanctity of Jesus,
  Sanctify me.
Purity of Jesus,
  Purify me.

Cross of Jesus,
Support me.
Nails of Jesus,
Hold me.
Mouth of Jesus,
Bless me in life, in death, in time and eternity.
Mouth of Jesus,
Defend me in the hour of death.
Mouth of Jesus,
Call me to come to Thee.
Mouth of Jesus,
Receive me with Thy saints in glory evermore.

Let us pray

Unite me to Yourself, O adorable victim. Life-giving heavenly Bread, feed me, sanctify me, reign in me, transform me to Yourself, live in me; let me live in You. Let me adore You in Your life-giving Sacrament as my God, listen to You as to my Master, obey You as my King, imitate You as my Model, follow You as my Shepherd, love You as my Father, seek You as my Physician who will heal all the maladies of my soul.

Be indeed my Way, Truth and Life; sustain me O heavenly Manna, through the desert of this world, till I shall behold You unveiled in Your glory. Amen.

This version of the Anima Christi *was composed by Saint Elizabeth Ann Seton on the Feast of Corpus Christi, 1816.*

CANTICLE OF BROTHER SUN

O most high, almighty Lord God,
To You belong praise, glory, honor and all blessings.

Praise to my Lord God with all His creatures,
And especially our brother the sun, who brings us the day
and who brings us the light;

Fair is he who shines with such great splendor;
O Lord, he signifies You to us!

Praise to my Lord for our sister the moon and for the stars,
Which He has set clear and lovely in heaven.

Praise to my Lord for our brother the wind, for air and
clouds, calms and all weather
By which You sustain life in all creatures.

Praise to my Lord for all those who pardon one another
for His love's sake,
And who endure weakness and tribulation;

Blessed are they who peaceably shall endure;
For You, O God, shall give them a crown!

Praise to my Lord for our sister, the death of the body
from which no man escapes.
Woe to him who dies in mortal sin!

Blessed are they who are found walking in Your most holy
will,
For the second death shall have no power to do them harm.

Praise and bless the Lord and give Him thanks,
And serve Him with great humility.

(St. Francis of Assisi)

A PRAYER FOR CHRISTIAN UNITY

Lord Jesus Christ, at Your Last Supper You prayed to the Father that all should be one.

Send Your Holy Spirit upon all who bear Your name and seek to serve You. Strengthen our faith in You, and lead us to love one another in humility.

May we who have been reborn in one baptism be united in one faith under one Shepherd. Amen.

Thou shalt not take the name of the Lord Thy God in vain.

THE GOLDEN ARROW
(A Prayer in Reparation for Blasphemy)

May the most holy, most sacred, most adorable, most mysterious and unutterable Name of God be always praised, blessed, loved, adored and glorified in Heaven, on earth and under the earth, by all the creatures of God, and by the Sacred Heart of our Lord Jesus Christ in the most Holy Sacrament of the altar.

This prayer was revealed by Our Lord to a Carmelite Nun of Tours in 1843 as a reparation for blasphemy.

"This Golden Arrow will wound My Heart delightfully," He said, "and heal the wounds inflicted by blasphemy."

Imprimatur
✠ *T. J. Toolen, Archbishop of Mobile-Birm.*

SPACE FOR YOUR FAVORITE PRAYERS

SPACE FOR YOUR FAVORITE PRAYERS

REFERENCE

TITLES OF SONG LIST AND AUTHORS

JESUS ROSARY:

1- His Peace is Flowing Like a River (*Rv. Carey Landry*—NALR)
2- City of God *(Rv. Dan Schutte SJ*—NALR)
3- All That I Am (*Sebastian Temple*)
4- We Gather Together (*Omer Westendorf*—WLP)
5- Spirit of the Living God (*Michael Iverson*)
6- He is Lord (*Author unknown*)
7- Look Beyond (*Darryl Ducote*)
8- Lord Send Out Your Spirit (*Joe Zsigray*—NALR)
After 9, and finish—All People That on Earth Do Dwell (*Louis Burgeois*)

JOYFUL

1- Immaculate Mary (*People's Hymnal*—WLP)
2- Sing a New Song (*Rv. Dan Schutte*—NALR)
3- O Come All Ye Faithful (18th Century, tr. *F. Oakeley*)
4- Go Tell it on the Mountain (*John Work Jr.*)
5- Here I Am Lord (*Rv. D. Schutte*—NALR)

SORROWFUL

1- I Have Loved You (*Michael Joncas*—NALR)
2- Sweet Sacrament We Thee Adore (*Author unknown*)
3- Lay Your Hands (*Rv. Carey Landry*—NALR)
4- Oh Lord I Am Not Worthy (Verse 1—*Anon.*)
5- Were You There (*Negro Spiritual*)

GLORIOUS

1- He Is Lord (*Author unknown*)
1- His Peace is Flowing Like a River (*Rv. Carey Landry*—NALR)
3- Come Holy Ghost (*Rabanus Maurus*)
4- I Lift Up My Soul (*Tim Manion*—NALR)
5- City of God (*Rv. D. Schutte*—NALR)

NALR - North American Liturgy Resources (*Glory and Praise Volumes*) Phoenix, AZ.

WLP - World Library Publications, Schiller Park, IL.

Refr: Fr. Gerard McGinnity, taken from: *Praying The Rosary With Our Lady, Queen of Peace*. Roman Press Ltd., Lurgan, Ireland.

THE RIEHLE FOUNDATION

The Riehle Foundation is a tax-exempt non-profit foundation distributing Catholic literature around the world. Since 1977, thousands of books, Bibles, rosaries, etc., have been sent free to missions and seminaries in third world countries, to hospitals, prison chaplains, etc.

The foundation is deeply committed to making known Our Lord's message of love and peace. Today it seems that message is being delivered to the world through Our Mother, Mary, at Medjugorje; a continuation of the Fatima message delivered in 1917.

The Riehle Foundation publishes several books on Medjugorje.

The Apparitions at Medjugorje Prolonged
    By Fr. René Laurentin ($5)

Latest News of Medjugorje—June 1987
    By Fr. René Laurentin ($4)

Our Lady of Medjugorje
    With full color photos.
    By Judith M. Albright ($3.50)

Our Lady Teaches About Prayer at Medjugorje
    By Fr. Albert J. M. Shamon ($1)

Messages and Teachings
    By Fr. René Laurentin ($7)
    The theology of Medjugorje

Copies may be ordered from THE RIEHLE FOUNDATION. Donations, though not required, are deeply appreciated. Suggested values for the above books are indicated.

Please write to:

THE RIEHLE FOUNDATION
P. O. Box 7
Milford, OH 45150

All contributions are used for the publishing and/or distribution costs of providing spiritual material to a world desperately in need of learning more about and living in God's peace and love.